THE

INTELLIGENT

GUIDE TO FAT

LOSS AND

MUSCLE

INTELLIGENT SHEDDER

First Edition
Published by The Intelligent Shedder

Berkshire, UK

Amazon Kindle Direct Publishing ISBN: 9798301623790

For more information, visit: https://intelligentshedder.com

CONTENTS

INTRODUCTION

The year is 1999 in a school sports hall in Berkshire. 100 boys are lined up along one wall in height order: smallest to tallest. I was one of them. I can still smell the varnish. I was one of the youngest boys in my year at school, therefore I was one of the smallest. Out of 100 boys I stood at the very far end, within the two or three shortest. Some of the other kids had ten and a half months on me. Ten and a half months of growing, developing skills and figuring it out. The sports master went down the line and split the year group into classes of thirty. If you had looked at that line-up and said that in 25 years' time someone in that line would be writing a book about fitness, you would never have bet it was me.

This is known as the relative age effect. According to a study from Grand Valley State University, Michigan, 36% of NHL draftees were born in the first quarter of the year. Only 14% of draftees were born in the last quarter of the year[1].

I have always loved sport; it was like modern warfare to me. Some of my earliest memories are of the 1996 Olympics and Euro '96. I was eight years old. I can remember just managing to stay awake to see England dumped out by Germany after penalties. Sport was how modern countries battled it out. It took strategy, teamwork, and skill. In stadiums and arenas, the biggest countries in the world fought for gold medals. Athletes are the modern-day warriors.

I loved playing sport too. I played a lot, but I also missed out on a lot. I was often picked last, if at all. If you don't get picked you don't get the same opportunities. I

---

[1] Deaner, R. O., Lowen, A., & Cobley, S. (2013). Born at the wrong time: selection bias in the NHL draft. PloS one, 8(2), e57753. https://doi.org/10.1371/journal.pone.0057753

had resigned to the fact that I was never to be an athlete. I came to accept that sporting ability was something you were either born with or you weren't. The talented few were blessed with the talents that could make them successful, rich, and famous.

Until one day when I was about sixteen years old my preconceptions were shattered. During a PE lesson at school, we were given a New York Times article from 1986 about John Naber. Naber was an American swimmer, five-time Olympic medallist, and wrote a book about goal setting. Naber was hugely successful in the seventies. Whilst my friends idolised David Beckham or Alan Shearer, my sporting idol was a swimmer few had heard of in the UK. What he said completely changed my perspective on talent. I took way more from this article than anything I had learned about goal setting before.

"John Naber, a 1976 Olympic gold medal winner in swimming, described how he developed a plan to win the 100-metre backstroke' in the 1976 Olympics while

watching the 1972 Olympics. He determined that he would need to lower his time four seconds in four years to win, a formidable task. However, he realised that if he trained 10 months or so per year, he would need to lower his time a tenth of a second per month, and by training six days a week, it would be only 1/300th of a second per day. He then figured he would need to improve a 1,200th of a second per hour of practice. A 1,200th of a second is less than the blink of an eye. If he could improve the equivalent of an eye-blink per workout, Naber could win the 100-metre backstroke in 1976. He did." - Steven J. Danish, New York Times, 1986.

At the time I thought John Naber had gone from a nobody watching the Olympics to a world record holding Olympic champion. This wasn't true, he was already in the US swimming team, but had been dropped from the 1972 Olympics. Everyone can make small progress in any area that compounds to seismic shift over several years. You could pick any goal, if you broke it down into small enough steps it was achievable. If the progress you can make is as small as the smallest increments you can break your goal down into, there's nothing you can't achieve. I learned that everything in sport was achievable. Talent was only where you started, but consistent hard work was the fuel that delivered you to your goal. Nothing is fixed, and everything is both figure-outable and achievable.

That's when I started lifting weights. I didn't have to compete against anyone else. I was competing against myself. I recorded everything I did. Every weight, every rep and every set. Very quickly the numbers started to go up. For the first time ever, I felt that everything was mine to create. Everything now was decided by the effort I put in. I may have started later or further back, but I was quickly overtaking people ahead of me. If I work harder than anyone else in the room. Eventually, people started asking me for advice. My coaching career began at nineteen working in the university gym. I took this mentality with me throughout my career. I got into university, studied sport and exercise science, did a Master's degree in sport psychology and got a job in professional sport.

I have read everything there is to read about training. I have hundreds of books on strength training, nutrition, endurance, bodybuilding, physiology, psychology and more. The more I read the hungrier I became for more knowledge. Anytime an author mentioned another book I dog-eared the page and made a list of all the other books they mentioned. My reading list grew. Everything I have put in my coaching I have taken from one of these books. Then combined it with something I learned in another book and turned it into something that is unique to me. I am a firm believer that every problem has a solution. Someone has already figured out the solution to your problem and written it in a book. You just must find it. Over the years I have whittled down everything I've ever absorbed and streamlined it into a very effective coaching system. I have taken some of the most technical principles of training, tested them in the gym

THE INTELLIGENT GUIDE TO FAT LOSS AND MUSCLE

with real people, and documented them. Here you can read them in a simple to understand format and take them away as if I am giving you a coaching session. I enjoy reading the latest science, it is my passion, not yours, you just want what works. This book took me over a year to write but is nearly twenty years in the making.

Everything in this book has been tested over years with thousands of real men just like you. It is a summary of my personal experiences, training, and coaching. My intention is to give you something pragmatic that will give you results in a less than perfect world.

There are three sections to this book: measurements, nutrition, and training. You can read the sections in any order you like. They are standalone sections with an action plan at the end of each chapter. Start where you like, highlight, write on the pages, make notes, dog-ear the pages, and do whatever you need to make the information stick.

In the first section I'll teach you how to gain clarity around what progress really looks like in terms of fat loss and muscle gain. You will be able to score your fitness like never before. You won't need any expensive or fancy equipment. Instead, you will get all you need with no more than a tape measure and some callipers you can get online. After reading this section, you stop having to guess whether you are making any real change or not, but instead create successful results. Giving yourself the blueprint to repeat great results every week. I put this section ahead of nutrition and training so that you can have your scorecard ready for when you start training and start measuring your results right away. If you can measure something, then you can change something. Too many people see their fitness as an 'either or'. I am currently unfit. If I train and eat right, then maybe one day I will be fit. By never clarifying what fit looks like or the steps it takes to get there, they get disheartened and give up long before achieving results. My goal is to remove that confusion and teach you the steps to take and how to tick off the milestones as you go.

Of course, this book would not help you burn fat and build muscle if it didn't have a section on nutrition. In the second section I'll give you the framework to do just this, not hope to achieve this by chance. My goal here is to give you the flexibility you need to get long lasting results within the guardrails of a healthy and effective nutrition plan. Chances are you know what it takes to get healthy. Like most, you have probably been distracted by the bullshit that is circulating. When you finally learn the mechanics behind fat loss and muscle gain you will come to realise that there are no shortcuts. Results can be produced and reproduced consistently once you know how.

Finally, we finish with the training section. Here you will get to create your own training plan, within the parameters that I set for you. My goal is to help you to fall in love with training. Let's face it when training isn't fun, you're not going to choose to stick to it for the long term. I have stripped it down into its fundamentals, so you can build an enjoyable and effective program. A lot of people get this part of training wrong. They think that training must be entertaining. There's a difference between entertaining and fun. Fun is enjoying the process and getting results. I've seen a lot of poorly structured programs where the trainer is just entertaining the client going nowhere. There is a time for playing around. My goal for you is the deeply satisfying feeling that you get when you see progress being made every week. I want you to get great results that you love, but most importantly I want you to learn how those results are created. Empowering you to fine-tune your training plan to accelerate your results even further.

This book is different because it's not a quick fix. Yes, you will get results quickly, but more importantly you will start seeing your body as a series of experiments. Once you have the fundamentals understood you can start to adjust your own program. Pulling the levers, turning the dials, and observing what happens. The point is not to follow diets aimlessly for the rest of your life, or 'working out' because you need to. It's figuring out what your body really wants, experimenting, and then enjoying the process. This is a more satisfying sense of play. Focus on mastering a few skills one week, then another set of skills the next week. There's no unlearning these skills once learned. Getting results becomes easier and easier as you know exactly what your body needs and how it responds.

Before you start, go to https://intelligentshedder.com/tools to get all the accompanying resources for this book. I have written all the plans you will need and they're yours free to access.

The following chapters have everything you need to get great results. I'd be wrong to think that any man could read a book and implement all the ideas right away without any issues. First, you need to understand the common obstacles that men face on this journey. Let's face it, if it were as simple as just following the strategies in this book you would already be there, right?

Let's discuss the common obstacles that derail the hundreds of men I have coached.

CHALLENGES

When I'm taking on new clients, I survey them to better understand the obstacles that they face. I've now surveyed hundreds of men and here are the five most common obstacles that I hear.

No clearly defined goal

If you were to fly from London to New York, you would fly on a heading of 258 degrees WSW. Fly 259 degrees WSW, however, and you will end up in Boston, MA, over 200 miles away from New York. It's the same in fitness; a clear goal is essential. You must know what the end-product looks like to achieve it. There are over twenty 'types' of fitness: strength, endurance, flexibility, etc.

Saying you want to be 'fitter' is not specific enough. Your goal needs to be so clear that you know exactly the next step you need to always take. This may sound obvious, but I've lost count of how many men have sought out my services, but when asked, cannot say what the 'thing' is. You must be able to attach a metric to whatever you want to change, otherwise you won't be able to monitor it changing. I can track my bank balance, but I can't track how I *feel* about my bank balance. You want to feel better about your physique. That's important, but you need an objective measure to tell you exactly how well you are progressing. Your goal is not only what you use as checkpoints, but it also serves as your main motivation. To be motivating it must inspire. Let's say I have two destination goals; one is to go on safari in Kruger National Park and the other is to go to the shops. Although the latter is far more realistic, it's not going to inspire me.

"The higher the goal, the greater the effort invested" –

Dr. Edwin Locke

So, you have defined your goal but how do you

increase your chances to a 95% success rate when the

going gets tough?

Going it alone

Have you heard of Bob Bowman? Phil Jackson?

Graham Henry? Alex Ferguson? Without these coaches

we wouldn't have Michael Phelps, Michael Jordan, Jonah

Lomu or David Beckham. When you try alone, who

knows if you give up or go home early? No one. Of

course, getting a training partner would help. When you

double up accountability with knowledge of an expert,

your results are pretty much guaranteed.

A study by The American Society of Training and

Development (ASTD) found that telling someone else

about your goal makes you sixteen times more likely to

achieve it. You are 95% likely to achieve your goal if you

set specific check-ins with an accountability partner. That's what I do with my clients. Every week they report back with the progress they're making, the wins they've achieved, and what obstacles they've experienced. Their results are compounded by celebrating the wins and strategizing to head-off future obstacles.

I have had many coaches myself in both fitness and business because I can get over disappointing myself. However, I don't want to let down a professional, particularly if it's a coach that I look up to. We all want to impress with what we can do; let's use it to our advantage.

We all think we don't have enough time to fit in everything we want to do, let's look at what the real issue with time is.

Poor time management

35% of people cite 'not enough time' as the reason that they don't get fitter. There is no way to create more time, so what needs to change is the priority of daily tasks that are stopping you getting results.

A study comparing HIIT (high-intensity interval training) and medium intensity cardio training (MICT) found that participants got leaner and fitter in as little as 10 minutes per day. A sixth of the workout time with MICT training. If getting fitter can be reduced to less than ten minutes per day, but the average person spends over three and a half hours scrolling on their phone, clearly it is a time prioritisation problem and not a time availability problem.

That brings me onto my next point. If you are an average Brit then you spend three and a half hours scrolling on your phone and four and a half hours watching TV. Before you try to add more behaviours into your daily routine like going to the gym, exercising outdoors, or preparing fresh healthy meals, you must make time.

To be more productive I suggest time-blocking. Plan out your day according to time blocks of fifteen to thirty minutes. How many time blocks will you spend watching TV or sitting scrolling on your phone? How many time-blocks can you free up for your new lifestyle?

This will take some organisation and discipline, so let's look at discipline in more detail next.

Instant gratification

A video went viral a few years ago where children were told if they resisted eating a marshmallow when an adult left the room, they could have two marshmallows when the adult returned. It was a cute video watching the kids struggle to fight the urge to eat the marshmallow. What most people don't know is that in the original experiment by Dr. Walter Mischel, the children that could delay gratification had higher self-worth and confidence, achieved more academically, had better coping skills and social skills and had fewer behavioural problems.

We are no different to these children. If you can say no to temptation, you will achieve more and be happier. In my opinion there is no better example of this than your own health and fitness. The day you do a workout is not the day you get fitter. Not only are the benefits of exercise delayed until after you have recovered, but it takes multiple bouts of exercise to make a difference. How many people would stick to it if they could see the results instantly? Our 'instant world' has destroyed our ability to prolong gratification until we have really earned it. Why spend months struggling in the gym when you can get the same dopamine hit by watching Netflix or eating a pizza delivered to your door?

You will face temptations that you will have to say no to to be successful. Don't invite these distractions into your world. Create an environment that supports your health pursuits, not an environment that makes it an uphill struggle. You will have to have a conversation with your loved ones about what you need from them to support you. This leads into our last obstacle.

Social pressure

Jim Rohn, motivational speaker, and writer of several books on motivation once said: "you are the average of the five people you spend the most time with". One of the most common obstacles my clients face is because of the people around them. I'm not recommending you get rid of the people dearest to you. However, you do need to understand how our drive to please those closest to us can become our biggest obstacle.

Solomon Asch was a social psychologist in America in the 1950s. He devised a simple test that has been recreated in several TV pranks. One such prank, on a candid camera style show, had the participant waiting for a lift. When the lift doors opened several stooges in the lift were facing the back wall. As the participant enters the lift and joins the stooges do you think they stood facing the front? The generally accepted correct way, or did they join the stooges and face the back? Often the participants would join in with the others in the lift for fear of not fitting in. Asch took it a step further and had four contestants taking part in a TV quiz show. The contestants were asked a series of simple questions. Each contestant had to answer openly. There was only one real contestant. Three of the contestants were stooges, who would conspire together against the genuine contestant. When the stooges answered incorrectly, how often do you think the genuine contestant would copy their answer? In 75% of the answers the genuine contestant would answer incorrectly, copying the stooges. When the contestants answered the questions alone, they would only answer 3% of the questions incorrectly.

We will sacrifice a lot, even our own health, to fit in with the in-crowd. Whether this is the popular people at work or our friends and family. Even give up on our goals or sacrifice our health. It will take a lot for us to go against what our peers are doing. We are social creatures after all.

You can use the power of social support to your advantage. Don't make this journey alone. Get a friend to be an accountability partner or start spending more time with people who have the same goals as you. You don't have to cut out people in your life, just redefine how you spend your time with them. Have that conversation with those people who have the greatest impact on your life. Explain what you are pursuing and how important their support is to you.

Note

If you are female and reading this book, the formulae we use in the following sections are written with men in mind. Do not fret, there are specific formulae for females at https://intelligentshedder.com/tools. Everything else you read will work just as well for you.

Now we're ready to get started. First, we need to take some measurements of where you are at currently. Then we can create a plan of how we are going to track your changes each week.

SECTION 1 -

MEASUREMENTS

The goal of this section is to set up a system of checks and balances. These will tell you if the nutrition and training strategies are working, and what changes to make if they are not.

Why do you take measurements? Measurements are taken when trying to change something. recognising that it has two components. The input of what you are doing and the output, the result you are trying to create. The measurements guide you on the input and tells you if you should be doing more or less of it. The output tells you if the changes you made are having an effect. And the feedback loop continues. When correctly done the feedback loop will rotate more efficiently each time. Most people understand measuring outputs. Few people effectively measure inputs. They are aware of whether they are achieving their goal or not, but they have no idea what is causing this. The obvious example is weight. How many people jump on the scales to see what their weight is (the output), but have no idea what input to change if it's not working? Measurements are taken poorly when this feedback loop is ignored. Often measurements are taken in isolation and to prove if what has already been done has worked. A sort of 'Are we there yet?' check. We tend to measure things in the start to see how far our starting point is away from the goal. What is the point in measuring in the first place if you don't know continue to measure and adjust frequently?

If the measurements that you are taking are telling you that you are not making any progress, then what you are doing is having *zero effect*. If the progress you are making is at half the rate that you expected. You need a measurement that will tell you how much to increase your inputs to double your outputs.

You would think someone is crazy if they measured progress in any other area like they did with measuring their fitness. You wouldn't judge the health of your finances by glancing at the balance of your bank account on any random day. You would clearly need the context of other things: assets, investments, savings, debt etc. as well as having a system to flatten out the peaks and troughs. More on this later.

Fitness being a word with the suffix *-ness* means the 'degree or condition of something'. If I said redness, I would be referring to how red something is, not necessarily whether it is red or not. So why when someone is talking about their fitness, they tend to say whether they are fit or not in absolute terms?

The problem is, we don't tend to act until something becomes so much of a problem that we are forced to act. We don't leave ourselves much time let alone time to properly come up with a plan before acting. We tend to try to go from zero to a hundred miles an hour a quick as possible. Our fitness only comes into our consciousness when we make ourselves aware of it. We forget that the thing we are measuring didn't come into existence the first day we started measuring it. In fact, it was always a 'thing' but by measuring it we are now it is us that is just looking at the barometer on it.

Weight is often measured as a proxy for fitness. We have been conditioned to believe that lighter always equals better. We don't like the way we look, move or feel so we try to conceptualise this by stepping onto the scales to give a score to our current state. Then if we lose an amount of weight from this, we assume that our state will change. But is lighter always better? Can you be both heavier and fitter?

When Usain Bolt broke the world records in both the 100m and the 200m, making him the fastest man on the planet, he reportedly weighed 94 kilograms. According to the Center for Disease Control and Prevention the average American man weighs 90.7 kilograms. Clearly weight alone is not a proxy for health. The measurements you use need to be sensitive to what they are measuring.

That is, the change in the measure accurately reflects a change in what you are trying to change. A change in weight could reflect a loss of fat tissue, but it could also reflect a loss of muscle tissue.

The tools I am going to give you aren't perfect in isolation. In fact, you could google each one and find the margin of error of a few percent and think what's the point in using them. You are taking measurements as a snapshot of something that is dynamic and in constant flux. Like checking the oil levels in your car as you drive it. The idea is not to achieve perfection with the measurements. Are we really concerned that the scales are accurate to the nearest 100g? If you are consistent with your measurements, less than perfect accuracy are replaced by the benefits of consistency. In the battle between accuracy and consistency, consistency always wins.

I use the following analogy to compare the difference between accuracy and consistency. I have two rulers; one is a metal ruler, and one is a fabric tape measure.

We can't guarantee that either was printed perfectly accurately in the factory. That what it says is one metre is one metre. However, the metal ruler won't deform over time, but the fabric tape measure may gradually stretch the more it is used. It will lack consistency compared to the metal ruler. Things will be measured consistently with the metal ruler but inconsistently with the fabric tape measure.

Consistency allows you to moderately adjust your behaviours (the things that you are doing) to adjust the results that you are getting. This will empower you to view what you are doing more objectively, stay on track and get back on track when you go slightly of course.

The idea is to use multiple measures to cross-check against each other. Rather than relying on one measure alone, use multiple measures. Swap weight alone for weight, waist circumference and body composition. I'll teach you how to do this in this section. Rather than assuming because your weight has or hasn't changed. I'm going to teach you to look a level deeper and understand what metrics signal that you are making real progress.

By using multiple measurements, I am now saying what is the probability that my fitness has improved if I am seeing the combination of effects. For example, my weight, waist circumference and body fat have all decreased. On the flip side, how likely is it that my fitness hasn't improved if these have all changed? Each factor that I include will confirm further that I am achieving my goal. Compounding the strength of the measurements I am taking. If several factors change positively, how much more likely is it that my fitness is improving?

The purpose of this section is to teach you how to monitor your progress. This will help you to make reasonable adjustments each week. The measures in this section are easy to understand and very simple to do yourself. They are accurate and sensitive enough to tell you if what you are doing is working. Highlighting a clear path to your end goal. I'll even teach you with a few little tweaks how to make them even more powerful!

Lack of clarity is the number one reason why people fail, quit, and return and try again and again. They can't be sure which inputs are creating which outputs, so they frantically try to change everything, before giving up.

Without expensive lab equipment, we rely on predictive models—mathematical equations that estimate values based on specific factors. In anthropometry, the study of human body measurements, some measurements can be complex, costly, or require specialised tools or expertise. However, when scientists use advanced tools like DEXA or MRI scanners to measure body fat percentage, they often identify simpler, easily measured factors that correlate with those results. It would be foolish not to use these simpler methods, as researchers have already done the hard work of testing them on thousands of participants to create reliable, "good enough" models.

Predictive Models

Sir Frances Galton - Charles Darwin's first cousin - was a Victorian scientist and philanthropist. Galton was very interested in genetics, which was a hot topic in Victorian Britain. He conducted an experiment using 70 sweet-pea seeds. He grew the seeds into plants and harvested the seeds from the plants. He then compared the sizes of the parent and offspring seeds. Galton discovered that although sweet peas were self-pollinating, and pass on all their genes to their offspring, the parents didn't create perfect clones of themselves. There was a relationship between the size of parent seeds and offspring seeds, but the size of the parent bean didn't 100% predict the size of the offspring beans. The size of the parent was the biggest factor, but not the only factor, that determined the size of the offspring. It was likely previous generations had diminishing effects on the size of the seeds from new plants. The parents largely predicted the size of the offspring, then the grandparents, then the great grandparents, *ad infinitum.*

What does this have to do with building a predictive model? If you have a large enough sample, you can find the percentage that each factor has on what you are investigating. In this example, the percentage effect parent size has on sweat-pea seeds, then grandparents and so on. To build a predictive model you find all the factors that affect the value you are trying to predict. You weigh them according to the effect size that they have. You can create a model that predicts the same in the future. If you know the factors that affect what you are investigating.

In anthropometry there are many things that have been investigated using predictive models. Let's take one of the most used equations in fitness, metabolism. We will look at this in more detail in the nutrition section, but for now it serves as the perfect example of a predictive model:

$Basal\ Metabolic\ Rate\ (BMR)$

$$= 5 + 9.9 \times Weight\ (kg)$$

$$+ 6.25 \times Height\ (cm) - 5 \times Age\ (years)$$

To directly measure metabolism, you need expensive specialist laboratory equipment. You wear a mask that measures the amount of air breathed in and out. Usually overnight whilst the participant sleeps in the lab. They then found the factors, weight, height, age and sex, that predict basal metabolic rate. If you look at the above formula, you can see how this predictive model works. When predicting BMR we start with 5 kcal at 0 kilograms of weight, 0cm of height and 0 years old. This is impossible, but this is a mathematical model. Then we add 9.9 kcal for every kilogram of weight he has and 6.25 kcal for every cm of height he has. These are positive predictors. That is that as weight and height increase so too does the amount of energy this man burns. Which makes sense, the heavier and taller the organism the more cells that require fuel. Then for every year of age we take away 5 kcal. As age increases basal metabolic rate decreases 5 Kcal per year. Weight being the biggest predictor of basal metabolic rate (9.9 kcal per kg), then height (6.25 kcal per cm), finally age (5 kcal per year). There are over a dozen similar formulae that will give similar results to within a few hundred kcal. They may not be perfectly accurate, but they are accurate enough to give a starting point to create a nutrition plan. As we will do later.

My goal is to keep this as simple as possible for you without the need for any expensive equipment or having to learn how to use it. Therefore, we will be using predictive models.

Where we cannot cut out and directly measure something, such as fat mass or muscle mass, we must estimate. It doesn't matter how big your budget you have there is no getting away from this point. Scientists still must estimate instead of directly measure, unless their participant is dead. They just have bigger and better machines to estimate than we do. Fortunately for us, there have been thousands of studies that have refined the factors that will predict what we are measuring. They have verified these variables and excluded others that are unimportant. I have built a measuring system that reflects this and I'm going to teach you how to use it.

It is important that you do not fall into old habits of focusing on one individual factor. Each factor on its own will not tell us everything we need to know. Together they combine to paint a highly detailed picture of body composition change. Scientifically, the difference between values is known as *variance*. If I am short and you are tall the difference between our height is the variance. We can then investigate the factors that predict that variance. Your parents might be taller than mine. Measurements can be vastly improved by stacking more factors. Take Body Mass Index (BMI) as one example. BMI isn't perfect because it is a crude measure of density by taking weight proportional to height (BMI = weight ÷ height^2), regardless of what that weight is composed of. So, a 100-kilogram athlete and a 100-kilogram obese person scored the same. However, it stacks the factor height with weight instead of using weight alone. Usain

Bolt may weigh more than the average American man, but his BMI (24.7) is significantly lower (29.3). BMI has been vastly improved by adding waist circumference with weight and height. I will now introduce a third man. This man is 188cm tall, so he is significantly taller than the average American (175cm). He weighs an incredible 118 kilograms; nearly thirty kilograms heavier than the average American. Would you say this man has an ideal physique or not? We can't be 100% sure, it could go either way. If we now add in another factor, such as waist circumference it might help. The average American has a waist circumference of 102.9cm, our mystery man has a waist circumference of 86 centimetres. Clearly this man is a fine specimen. You may have already guessed he is of course Arnold Schwarzenegger in his prime. By stacking more factors, we are saying what's the probability that a person of x weight, y height and z waist circumference is either an athlete or an obese person. The more factors we stack, the clearer our picture becomes. Try this out yourself, google some athletes and their stats and start to build a mental model of ideal physiques.

Back to your measurements. You will be a case study of one. The variance you will be measuring, won't be between you and someone else. It will be the difference you see each week in yourself as you move towards your goal. There will be seven factors that will predict your fat mass. We are asking what are the odds that if all these factors improve for the better that your fat mass has reduced? Pretty likely.

If you think back to our ruler versus tape measure analogy. I am not worried that my estimations aren't perfect, as long as the way that I measure them is reliable week in, week out. If you'd like to get your body composition or basal metabolic rate scientifically estimated, then go for it. I'd still recommend using my measures to track progress weekly rather than a one-off snapshot. The other reason we take measurements regularly is so that it will shape our behaviours. We're not shutting the stable door after the proverbial horse has bolted. Taking measurements once a week will help you set short term goals and habits for that week. Do your measurements paint a detailed enough picture to guide your short-term decision making?

None of the measurements you are going to take are in and of themselves the be all and end all. There is no one number that can tell you exactly how healthy or fit you are. And not only that but we will not look at any single measure on its own at one moment in time. But compare the change in that number over days, weeks, or months. That if given x, y and z we assume that you are fitter or healthier than before.

The purpose of this section is to teach you how to create your own feedback loop of measurements. These measures will be sensitive enough to show whether your actions are producing the desired effects. They will also detect the impact of any adjustments you make, allowing you to maintain a continuous feedback loop to help you stay on track and achieve your goals.

You will learn:

1. How to track the changes in your weight

2. How to estimate your fat mass

3. How to discover how much muscle you have

4. How to measure fat loss specifically and,

5. which muscles or areas of growth to focus on to look amazing.

First, if you haven't already, go to https://intelligentshedder.com/tools. Download all the tools that I use and will be referring to from here on out. Every formula is here in the book, but if you go to the tools page you will get all the spreadsheets already completed for you.

Let's look at weight first and how to revolutionise how to track it.

.

WEIGHT

Weight alone is not a good snapshot of your current health. Using weight as a single measure to understand how healthy you are is wildly inaccurate. As we've already established. Instead, and if there is one lesson you take from this chapter, weight is a great tool to track over time, but a poor metric used on its own as a snapshot.

When we talk about weight, and referring to scale weight, what we are talking about is the weight of everything. The weight you see on the scales is your total body weight. Later in this section we will talk about the weight, also called mass, of different things. Some of these are signs of health when they decrease. Others are a sign of health when they increase. Being able to distinguish between these different masses is important, or things will get blurry. Nonetheless, it is still important to start with total body weight.

Focusing on total body weight alone leads to poor goal-setting and poor goal setting leads to failed goals. The traditional way to set a weight loss goal as an either/or goal "I am this weight, but I should/want to be this". Usually, the goal is to be one or two stone, or five or ten kilograms, less. Setting a goal to lose a stone is like setting a goal to earn a million pounds. The value of the label associated with the goal means more than the outcome of achieving the goal. Making it unlikely to be achieved. In my experience, 99% of people who set the goal to lose a stone haven't calculated that a stone is in fact what they should lose. They have a desire not to be the weight they currently are because it represents how they currently feel about their body.

The pitfall of setting goals like this is thinking you're setting a goal that is a specific and number-based goal.

Really, you're just stating what you don't want to be repeatedly. "I don't want to be the current weight that I am". I either achieve weight loss or I don't. Those are the two categories, either success or failure. They don't see the scale of weight loss and how it changes over time. It was changing before you went to the gym, and it will continue to change after you've stopped going to the gym. If we will always have mass, then we should lose our attachment to it. It is not the be all and end all when we are training, because it doesn't end. Let's just say that choosing to be ten kilograms less in weight is a good goal. You would have to be able to plan how to lose the first kilogram, then repeat the steps ten times rather than fixate on why you haven't lost ten kilograms yet. Writing-off the first nine kilograms lost until you achieve the tenth kilogram of weight loss.

We don't view making progress in other areas like we view making progress physically. If I were learning a language, I wouldn't wait until I was fluent in the language before I recognised that I had achieved levels of mastery.

If I was learning French, I would be happy after learning to count to ten, then the colours, then some simple greetings, then some phrases I can use and so on. I wouldn't wait until I had learned all 100,000 words of the French language before I considered that I had succeeded at learning French.

Most people start exercising and they take weight loss as a proxy for fat loss. This can be true a lot of the time when total weight loss reflects fat loss. When you include resistance training when trying to lose fat, the gains in lean mass can mask the amount of fat loss. When you are weighing yourself on a set of scales the scales are telling you the total mass of whatever is placed on top of it. In this instance it's your total body weight. If you stand on the scales holding a cookie you will weigh the same as if you stand on the scales once you have eaten the cookie. Overall weight does not distinguish between what is on top of it. If you drink a litre of water, you will weigh one kilogram heavier as a litre of water = a kilogram. The opposite is also true. If you are dehydrated by 1% of body weight, then you will weigh 1% less purely because of the reduced fluid levels in your body. At a total body weight this will give a false positive of -1 kilogram.

I am not teaching you this to further fuel the mistake I see even fitness professionals make when results are not as expected. We assign our success to the things we do and our failures to those outside of our control. Weight goes down, it must be the new diet and training regime. Weight goes up and it must be water retention or any other plethora of justifications. Instead, the purpose of the above is to illustrate that weight is a useful measure, of weight. We need to delve deeper to understand what is causing the changes in weight. Weight is only useful if it can be measured consistently and if you can distinguish the different types of mass that you have. Understanding the underlying mechanisms will help you to achieve successful fat loss. Weight loss might indicate fat loss and in most cases it does, in some cases it doesn't. Weight is the most basic measurement we will use, which means we won't ignore it, far from it, but instead treat it as such. It is the first, and most basic measurement before we delve deeper into the other measurements. In terms of painting the picture of our health, weight is like the blue wash for the sky. It's the first thing that goes on and the detailed picture is built on top. We still need to measure weight loss as total body mass loss. This number will then feed into the other numbers in our calculations.

The problem with monitoring weight only, is not an issue with weight itself as a metric, but how it is measured. A metric used poorly is not a poor metric. Weight tends to get measured at the extremes. When one knows it will either be 'bad', or 'good'. Typically used as punishment to see how bad things have gotten. If the former helps to kick start your motivation to act, then fine, so be it. Just be sure to drop this habit when you want to measure your progress successfully. If it is the latter, then good luck measuring progress in week two. You can only play that card once. Later I will show you a better way to 'score' your weight loss progress. First, I want to show you how to measure it more accurately. I haven't weighed any of my clients for years. This is because I see clients at all different times of day. Who knows how much mass of food and drink they've consumed during the day? As well as whether this is anywhere near the same amount that they ate or drank the previous day. The intelligent way to weigh-in is to take a trailing 7-day average. Instead of sporadically seeing a snapshot of where your total body weight is at any one moment in time. Weigh yourself from a few times a week up to daily, leave no more than a one-day gap, then you keep a rolling 7-day average. To avoid any false measurements, take your weight first thing in the morning, undressed, before eating or drinking anything, and after going to the toilet. Then record your weight in a spreadsheet and take the average of the last 7 days including today. This makes individual weight measurements irrelevant and flattens any fluctuations. These fluctuations will have a much smaller effect on your weight than if you happened to weigh yourself during a peak or trough.

An increase over 24 hours of 1kg would be spread across the seven days. The equivalent to an increase of 150g per day.⬚Kept in context with the other six days that may be down by more or less than 150g.

fx	=AVERAGE(B2:B8)		
A	B	C	D
Date	**Weight**	**T7DW**	**CHO**
01/07/2024	85.0	85.0	
02/07/2024	84.2	84.6	
03/07/2024	84.6	84.6	
04/07/2024	84.4	84.6	
05/07/2024	84.4	84.5	
06/07/2024	84.0	84.4	
07/07/2024	83.8	=AVERAGE(B2:B8)	

It stops any freak-outs over a single measurement. This is what is really happening inside your body. Your body isn't cashing in its fat reserves every evening when you go to bed. Any single weight measurement isn't terminal, in fact it is just a snapshot of a system that is in constant flux. Look at the image above and you can see how the trailing average in column C a much more flattened version of the raw data in column B.

The message in this chapter is that weight will tell you the overall trend of your body mass. The detailed picture is what is happening within that change. Is it an increase in lean mass, a decrease in fat mass or a combination of the two? All of which would be positive situations, not clear by looking at overall weight.

The goal here is not to set any total body weight goals until we have looked at body composition. Instead, we will come back to weight once we have determined a fat loss goal not a weight loss goal.

Action Points

1. Download the weight tracking tool at https://intelligentshedder.com/tools and start tracking your weight the intelligent way.

Next, let's add another measurement to weight to give it real power.

PROPORTIONS I

The example of Bolt and Schwarzenegger compared to the average American should show that we first need a simple measure to discriminate between those with high fat mass and high muscle mass. Fortunately, this can be done very simply.

We are now going to start looking at levels of adiposity. Adiposity is the amount of fat mass is stored in the body and is different to obesity. Obesity is used to describe the amount of body weight. Those who have a BMI above 25 kg/m^2 are classed as overweight whereas over 30 kg/m2 would class someone as obese, irrespective of the composition of that weight. Adiposity doesn't have these broad categories. Instead, adiposity can be described as body fat either as a percentage or in kilograms. More on this in the next chapter where I will show you how to set specific goals using body fat mass as a key metric. Some of these measures will use waist circumference to determine body fat. For now, we are going to use waist circumference to measure abdominal fat. Waist circumference is a good indicator of general adiposity and overall health because it is a relatively direct measure of abdominal adiposity. There is little muscle mass stored around the abdomen. The muscle that is stored there is unlikely to hypertrophy (grow) as much as other larger muscles. The variance in waist circumference will be dependent on the amount of fat stored around the abdomen. A larger waist circumference is indicative of greater abdominal fat storage, correlated to poorer health outcomes related to higher adiposity[2]. A good standard for waist

---

[2] Agbaje A. O. (2024). Waist-circumference-to-height-ratio had better longitudinal agreement with DEXA-measured fat mass than

circumference is half of your height. If you are six feet tall (182cm) you should have a waist circumference of approximately 91cm. A waist circumference greater than 99cm irrespective of height is related to a four to five-fold increase in risk of cardiovascular disease[3].

This gives another dimension to measuring our health. We can now consider weight, height, and adiposity. How heavy someone is versus how tall they are versus how large their abdomen is, paints a much better picture. Before, you probably only measured your weight, you are now scoring your health as your weight and waist proportional to your height.

Whenever we compare two factors, we create a matrix of four possible outcomes. In this instance we have high and low body mass with high and low fat mass. This gives four possible scenarios. We have those who have above

---

BMI in 7237 children. Pediatric research, 10.1038/s41390-024-03112-8. Advance online publication.

[3] Suwała, S., & Junik, R. (2024). Body Mass Index and Waist Circumference as Predictors of Above-Average Increased Cardiovascular Risk Assessed by the SCORE2 and SCORE2-OP Calculators and the Proposition of New Optimal Cut-Off Values: Cross-Sectional Single-Center Study. Journal of clinical medicine, 13(7), 1931. https://doi.org/10.3390/jcm13071931

average weight such as Usain Bolt, Arnold Schwarzenegger and many other athletes who also have low fat mass. These are in the top left of the below illustration. Then we have those with high body mass with high fat mass. These are the obese who would have a high or very high BMI, and this is due to high fat mass. As weight increases due to higher fat mass this closely correlates to a higher risk of heart disease, type two diabetes, and some cancers. Then we have those with low body weight. Continuing clockwise round the below illustration are those with low body weight and high fat mass. This is casually referred to as 'skinny fat' and indicates low activity and low muscle mass but an accumulation of some fat mass with overall low body weight.

As you learned in the previous chapter, total body weight is a poor predictor of health because it is too broad a measure. Waist circumference predicts the likelihood of obesity-related illnesses such as hypertension, cardiovascular disease, and some cancers.

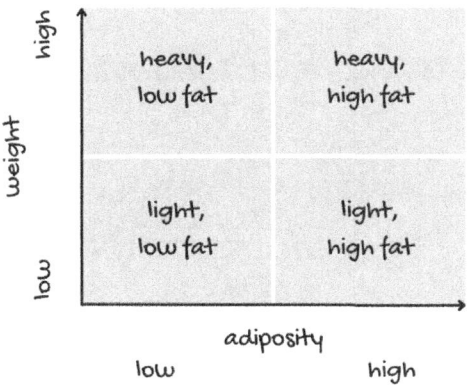

To measure your waist circumference, measure your waist at the midpoint between the top of your hip bone and the bottom of your ribcage. This is usually the narrowest point of your abdomen.

The size of your waist circumference can be called conicity. Put bluntly, it is the degree to which your trunk represents a cone with a larger bottom than top. In science this is known as conicity index (CI). A higher conicity index represents greater abdominal fat with increased risk of poor health. This is because more fat mass is stored around the organs. Looking at the equation below you can see that you don't necessarily need to calculate your conicity index. You must measure your waist circumference and your weight. Aim for the rule of 50% of height and no greater than 99cm.

$$Conicity\ Index\ (CI) = \frac{Waist\ Circumference\ (m)}{0.109 \times \sqrt{\dfrac{weight\ (kg)}{height\ (m)}}}$$

What is useful to understand here is the difference between a measurement and a calculation. Your height, weight and waist circumference are measurements. Your BMI, waist to height ratio, waist to hip ratio etc. are all calculations. You take measurements to create calculations, but the measurements themselves have value. An increase in waist circumference will negatively affect any calculation it is used in. Therefore, there is a lot of value in measuring waist circumference itself and noting if it has increased. You don't have to put this into any calculations to know this. Calculations are used because they help us visualise what we are trying to achieve. A waist approximately half of your height is a great visual representation. Measuring your waist circumference alone each week is helpful to monitor your progress.

Once you have measured your waist circumference you can compare it to several other measurements to make a comparison. As we already have, we can look at your waist circumference in relation to your height. Stature is a general indicator of your frame (skeleton) size. As people get taller their waist circumference also increases proportionally.

There are two more specific measurements we can use as benchmarks to compare against your waist circumference. Your chest and your hips. Your chest is expected to be the largest. At best 1.3 times greater than your waist and your hips 1.1 times greater than your waist. Your waist should be the smallest of the three. If your waist is the biggest; first aim to get your waist circumference within your chest circumference. Then aim to get your waist circumference within the circumference of your hips. How to achieve these will be covered in detail in the diet and training sections. To measure your hip circumference, take the tape measure and wrap it around your hips at the widest point on the outside of your hips. Measure your chest circumference by wrapping the tape measure around your chest at the widest point. Take the measurement after a normal exhalation. This gives you an initial indication of your body proportions. These three measurements give us a general model of the shape of your body. Either a cylinder where all the measurements are the same, a cone with the centre (waist) narrower than the top (chest; low conicity) or a cylinder with the centre wider than the top (high conicity).

You are now starting to put together a pretty good picture of health that goes beyond just weight. The initial goal, for waist circumference, is to achieve a waist circumference less than both chest and hip circumferences. We will take another look at proportions later but turn the focus on muscle size and use proportions to guide our muscle-building goals.

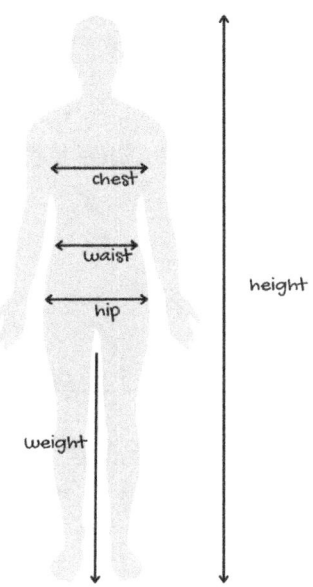

This is a good start for fat loss, and this will give you plenty to start with. In the next chapter I will teach you how to take your waist circumference and combine it with other measures to get an estimation of your fat mass. If you want to get clearer, you need to start thinking about the degrees of fat mass. This is where body composition in terms of body fat percentage and fat mass.

Action Steps

1. Measure your chest, waist, and hip circumferences.

2. Is your waist circumference close to 50% of your height?

3. Is your waist circumference less than your hip and chest circumference?

Next, I'll show you how to calculate your body composition with nothing more than a tape measure.

BODY COMPOSITION

The proportion of fat mass in your body relative to your weight is known as your body composition. This is often shown as a percentage; the percentage of your total mass that is fat mass. For example, an 80-kilogram man with a body composition of twenty percent has 16 kilograms of fat mass.

Body composition is always an estimate, a calculation if you remember from the previous chapter. There is no way of extracting and counting the fat mass in your body. Therefore, it is always taken with a grain of salt. As it's an estimate there is always a degree of error. This makes it unreliable to take as a single accurate calculation.

Combined with other measurements and tracked as a trend over time is useful.

Body composition from the scientific process of measuring the density of different objects which is over a thousand of years old. Archimedes was a scientist in the ancient city of Syracuse in Greece. One day he was sought out by the king of Syracuse who suspected the royal jeweller of ripping him off with a crown made of impure gold. Archimedes struggled to create a test where he could establish the percentage of gold in the crown. Until, it is said that whilst bathing at the local bathhouse he was observing men getting in and out of the water and the water level rising and falling. The water level rising and falling was due to the different volumes, i.e., the volume of water they displaced, of the men, rather than their weight. Two men of the same weight with different densities would displace different amounts of water. He celebrated this discovery by running home through the streets before getting dressed shouting "Eureka!".

Archimedes took the crown and the same weight of pure gold and compared how much water each displaced. If the crown was made of pure gold, it would displace the same amount of water as the crown. Any less than pure gold and the crown would displace more water. In fact, if he knew what other metal, such as silver, the crown was mixed with he could even establish what percentage of gold and silver the crown was.

To this day we use the same method to establish body fat percentage. This tells us the percentage of fat mass, and non-fat mass. We are simplifying body mass into two compartments. By knowing the density of body fat, 0.9g per cm^3, or 900g per litre. and the density of muscle, 1.1g per cm^3 or 1,100g per litre of volume we can determine body fat percentage. This is still done by weighing in water, known as hydrostatic weighing, which is the gold standard of body composition analysis. Other, more precise methods have been established such as dual X-ray absorptiometry and MRI scanning. Some cheaper and simpler methods have been developed and calibrated against the more precise methods. Allowing you to easily estimate your own body composition without the need for expensive equipment. Later in this chapter I will show you how.

It is important to remember that body composition is a calculation and is entirely conceptual. It is a visualisation of the percentage of your mass that is fat mass. Of course, things are never quite this simple. Lean mass is the name given to describe everything else inside the body (lean mass = total body mass minus fat mass). If you are 20% body fat, then you are 80% lean mass. Using our previous example, with a body weight of 80kg and body fat of 16kg means a lean mass of 64kg. This will become important later. The fluid stored in your body would be classed as lean mass however both lean mass and fat mass contain varying amounts of fluid. From person to person and within a person from day to day. To get a calculation that is perfectly accurate and reliable will be impossible. However, it is still a good enough illustration. In the next section I'll first show you how to estimate your body composition. Then, I'll show you how to make use of the measurements that go into the calculations as standalone measurements.

There are ideal targets for body fat percentage, but these aren't perfect. Instead, just like weight, body composition should be used as an individual tracking tool. It is much better to track changes in body fat over time rather than try to estimate accurately what your body fat is at any moment in time.

Men have around 3% essential fat, this is fat that is required physiologically for essential function. Fat is essential in the function of muscle, central nervous system, hormones and more. If body fat gets too low, then hormones become noticeably suppressed. This is seen in natural bodybuilders who achieve extreme levels of leanness suppressing natural testosterone levels[4].

---

[4] Schoenfeld, B. J., Androulakis-Korakakis, P., Piñero, A., Burke, R., Coleman, M., Mohan, A. E., Escalante, G., Rukstela, A., Campbell, B., & Helms, E. (2023). Alterations in Measures of Body Composition, Neuromuscular Performance, Hormonal Levels, Physiological Adaptations, and Psychometric Outcomes during Preparation for Physique Competition: A Systematic Review of Case Studies. Journal of functional morphology and kinesiology, 8(2), 59. https://doi.org/10.3390/jfmk8020059

An athletically lean physique is typically one that has a single-digit body fat percentage. I'll often set a goal for clients to aim for 9% body fat by losing body fat in 5% chunks from wherever they are starting from and reassessing at each milestone. 25% to 20% body fat is a visibly noticeable difference, so too is 14% to 9%. Everybody's journey is different, what is important is that a goal is set and strived for, rather than *being* a certain body fat percentage. Remember, body fat percentage is entirely conceptual. What do you achieve by being leaner? Has your health and happiness improved? And will it be improved more by aiming again for a lower body fat percentage?

Before setting a body fat percentage goal, it's important to understand where you are currently, as well as the timeframe to achieve your goal.

Next, we will look more specifically at how to calculate your fat mass and body fat percentage.

FAT MASS

There are no ways of directly measuring body fat. To do that we would have to be able to cut out the fat and weigh it. Which is clearly not possible. Instead, we take a series of measurements around the body that will predict the mass of fat in your body.

If you use magnetic resonance imaging, you are taking a series of pictures and estimating the mass of fat in the body. The measurements you will be taking have been verified against such more accurate methods, and for what we are trying to achieve, are good enough. You are taking these measurements to guide your decision making for training and nutrition. Do we keep doing what we are doing or do we increase or decrease something (more on training and nutrition in their respective chapters).

I don't use bioelectrical impedance machines that predict fat mass because they don't give a usable raw measure. They send an electronic signal through the body, measuring the resistance that signal experiences, in ohms. I can't picture the difference in different levels of resistance in ohms and it doesn't really help me with my training. Instead, I use measures that rely on a tape measure and skinfold callipers. The tape measure and skinfold callipers give you a reading in centimetres or millimetres. Measuring less will show that fat mass is being lost. I will use these measurements in their raw form without turning them into a body fat percentage. Measuring the skinfold thickness at different sites on the body will tell you just as much as a body fat percentage will. Halve the skinfold thickness of your abdominals from 30 to 15 millimetres, that's a quantifiable change that you can see.

In the last chapter you used waist circumference as a good measure of adiposity. Therefore, you will continue to use waist circumference as your measure as you are already collecting it. Now you are going to put it in a formula devised by the US Navy to assess recruits.

Prior to WWII servicemen were assessed purely on their performance measures. But after WWII as roles changed and the military was now very different to how it was previously; they needed a new way to assess recruits. BMI was originally used but due to its flaws mentioned earlier, needed to be replaced by something more accurate. It could be done at sea or in the field and could discern between fat mass and lean mass. Is a recruit heavy because they have a large amount of muscle or are they out of condition?

The US Navy generated a formula to estimate fat mass and all you need to use these formulae is a tape measure. I have created a spreadsheet for you to download so you don't have to worry about inputting the data. You can use my spreadsheet in a matter of minutes.

The test requires the waist circumference you have previously measured. In addition to your neck circumference. Measured where you would wear a collar, just below the Adam's apple. The formula uses the difference between your waist and neck circumference to measure adiposity. A positive weighting is given to those with larger lean mass and therefore larger necks. There will be more variability in waist circumference between leaner and less lean individuals. Less variability in neck circumference between lean and less lean individuals. A greater difference in waist and neck circumference would imply a greater body fat percentage. Height is also used in a similar way to how we used the waist to height ratio, that waist circumference is relative to stature. We are again thinking in terms of probabilities. What is the probability that someone who is heavier, but with a larger neck circumference and smaller waist circumference is fitter than someone of the same weight but a larger waist circumference? Pretty high. Here is the formula devised by the US Navy. If you'd rather just input your numbers into a spreadsheet and get your body fat percentage then download the tracker tool at https://intelligentshedder.com/tools.

As this formula was created in the USA the measurements are in inches rather than cm. You will need to convert your measurements from cm to inches. Multiply your circumferences by 0.394 to get inches. Or just check both sides of the tape measure!

$$US\ Navy\ BF\% = 86.01 \times \log_{10}(Waist - Neck) - 70.041 \times \log_{10}(Height) + 36.76$$

Your height will not change. Your neck circumference will remain relatively stable. The only factor that is likely to change significantly is your waist circumference. You can infer from this that a reduction in waist circumference will directly correlate to dropping body fat. Over a 90-day period a neck circumference may drop by an inch, but

I've seen men cut their waist circumference by 30% or more. Waist circumference is useful as a standalone measure. Conceptually, it helps put the measurement in context by using body fat percentage to turn this measure into something that can be easily visualised.

Each measurement can be put into a calculation to paint a picture of your health that can be tracked over time. I use both formulae, because I take the same measures for the same thing and take the average. I've had clients who have measured higher in body fat in one test and lower in another because of their proportions and where they store fat. In a sense, hedging on the average of the two being more reliable. You will see this method repeated later. This is like getting multiple professional opinions. Each calculation adds to the overall picture to give a more consistent reading.

The other way to estimate your fat mass is to use skinfold callipers. These are callipers that will measure the thickness of the skin and the layer of fat underneath it. This is done by taking a 'pinch' and pulling the subdermal fat away from the underlying muscle and connective tissue. The thicker this layer is, the greater your body fat. All mammals store excess fat under their skin. This provides a layer of insulation and protection. Animals will gradually increase their fat stores over the summer months when food is abundant in preparation for the cold winter where food is less plentiful, and temperatures drop. Body fat is not only a storage of extra calories, even though that is how it is gained. Our bodies have evolved over millions of years and haven't adapted to the omnipresence of highly palatable and calorie dense foods. We don't go through cycles of higher and lower body fat like other mammals. Instead, we experience a gradual drift upwards in body fat stores over time.

You can take measurements from two to eleven sites on the body to measure skinfold thickness. I'm going to give you the only two tests that use three sites. All three of these sites are on the front of the body and are easily reachable, allowing you to do them yourself.

If you would like the full list of tests, go to https://intelligentshedder.com/tools, but you will need a partner to measure the harder to reach sites. The equivalent tests for females have also been included on the above link. You will need a partner because all the tests use the back of the arm which you will not be able to measure yourself.

The three sites that you will be measuring are the chest, stomach, and thigh. This gives you the total of the three sites. The measurements are in millimetres and are of the layer of skin plus the layer of fat folded over. The actual depth from the surface of the skin to the bottom of the layer of fat is half this number.

The abdominal and the thigh fold are the easier as they are taken vertically. The finger and thumb of your right hand will pinch from three o'clock and nine o'clock to create the vertical fold. With the callipers in your left hand, make sure you have the callipers the right way up so you can easily see the ruler. Place the ends of the callipers so they are halfway up the fold of skin, so they measure where the skinfold is flattest, to give you a more accurate reading. Let the callipers come to a rest on the thickness, you can take the measurement a couple of times if you want to be sure. The sight of the abdominal measurement is level with the belly button but 3cm to the right-hand side of the body.

The site for the thigh is exactly halfway between the fold of the hip and the centre of the kneecap. You can establish this quickly using a tape measure. Again, using a vertical fold the same way you did for the abdomen.

The chest is taken exactly halfway between the nipple and the start of the arm pit. Use a tape measure to quickly find this point. The chest measurement, unlike the abdominal and the thigh measurement, is a diagonal measurement. Use the same method as the vertical pinch but rotate it 45 degrees to make a diagonal. The fold is along the same line as a seat belt would be if it were going over the shoulder and across the body, out from the shoulder down and into the body. You will find a way where the skin will naturally want to fold in your hand when you make a pinch.

You can get two different styles of skinfold calliper. One style like tongs and clicks when they meet resistance, and the measurement is marked with a slide along the ruler. The other types are like a large set of pliers that use a scissor action, so you squeeze them open. These are very simple to use and can be bought cheaply online. The cheap sets are perfect for using on yourself. Don't feel like you must invest in an expensive set. A cheap set will work perfectly for measuring yourself regularly with the three sites.

Take the total of the three sites and put the total into the following formula. For example, if your chest is 10mm, your abdomen is 24mm and your thigh is 8mm your 'sum of skinfolds' is 42mm. You will also have to square this number for the second part of the equation.

$$\%BF = 495 \div \big(1.10938$$

$$- (0.0008267 \times Sum\ of\ Skinfolds)$$

$$+ (0.0000016$$

$$\times Sum\ of\ Skinfolds\ Squared)$$

$$- (0.0002574 \times Age\ in\ years)\big) - 450$$

For the previous example, we enter the skinfold total as the sum of skinfolds, not forgetting to square it the second time and add your age, let's take the example of 40 years old.

$$\%BF = 495 \div \big(1.10938 - (0.0008267 \times 42)$$

$$+ (0.0000016 \times 42^2) - (0.0002574 \times 40)\big)$$

$$- 450 = 15\%$$

The next formula combines the sum of the same three skinfolds. We combine these three skinfolds with waist circumference. I'm now going to introduce another circumference, forearm circumference. Forearm circumference is used in the same way that neck circumference was used in the US Army and Navy test. This will positively discriminate those with larger muscle mass. Larger muscle mass is measured by larger forearms rather than larger necks. To measure your forearm circumference, wrap the tape measure around the thickest part of your forearm. Make sure you convert your waist and forearm measurement to metres before inputting them into the formula. If you measure them in mm multiply by 1,000 or if you use cm multiply by 100. As before, you will use both the sum of your skinfolds and the sum of your skinfolds squared.

$$%BF = 495 \div \big(1.099075 - (0.0008209 \times 42)$$
$$+ (0.0000026 \times 42^2) - (0.0002017 \times 40)$$
$$- (0.005675 \times 0.815)$$
$$+ (0.018586 \times 0.035)\big) - 450 = 15\%$$

Using the previous example again, we enter the skinfold total as the sum of skinfolds, not forgetting to square it the second time and add your age, again I'll use 40 years old as the age and I'll use a waist circumference of 81.5 cm (0.0815 m) and a forearm circumference of 35 cm (0.035 m).

$$\%BF = 495 \div (1.099075$$
$$- (0.0008209 \times Sum\ of\ Skinfolds)$$
$$+ (0.0000026$$
$$\times Sum\ of\ Skinfolds\ Squared)$$
$$- (0.0002017 \times Age\ in\ years)$$
$$- (0.005675$$
$$\times Waist\ Circumference\ in\ metres)$$
$$+ (0.018586$$
$$\times Forearm\ Circumference\ in\ metres))$$
$$- 450$$

Some people will score higher on some measures and lower on others. To insure against this, I take all measurements and use the average to give me a more stable number that won't bias one formula over another.

Measuring your waist circumference and the sum of the three sites for skinfolds will give you more direct measurements. I'm more concerned with any change of waist circumference and skinfolds than the body fat percentage. The second formula for body composition uses the skinfold measurements with the circumference of the waist and forearm. This separates those with greater muscle mass and increases the power of the measurement. I have six measurements I can look at (weight included) rather than having a machine churn-out just body fat percentage.

If you think about how these measures will change, just like the US Army and Navy formulae, you know what measures you are looking for changes in. Just like neck circumference, forearm circumference will stay relatively stable over several weeks. It may increase by a centimetre or two, but this will only improve our body fat score further. A successful plan will see your waist circumference and each of your skinfolds decrease significantly. You will be able to see a slimmer waist and thinner skin covering your muscles, increasing your muscle tone. This is where abdominal fat gets the reputation of being 'stubborn'. Abdominal fat is not stubborn, it is the same as any other body fat. Your body naturally will store more fat around your organs as a layer of protection. Your body is not designed to store as much body fat as the modern world is making it so it still distributes fat in the same ratios. Once you have taken your own skinfolds you will see that your abdominal skinfold thickness is likely the greatest. If you lose 1 mm from each site per week, it will take longer to lose enough fat from your abdomen to see visible change. Let alone the six pack you may want to reveal. Your abdomen does not refuse to relinquish fat. You will just see your thigh and your chest 'bottom out' before you see your abdomen reach its potential. Many people give up long before this happens and never see the toned stomach that is just as possible as toned arms or legs. It just takes more patience.

I rarely use bioelectrical impedance machines to estimate body fat. Although they are quick to deliver the final body fat percentage. They don't give me direct measurements I can track myself to keep my finger on the pulse weekly.

Once you have your body fat percentage you can multiply your total body mass by the percentage to give you an estimation of fat mass in kilograms. This gives you clearer training and nutrition goals. You now know how many kilograms of fat mass you have and want to lose. You can set a specific goal to achieve a certain body fat percentage or losing a certain amount of fat mass.

If we take the above example of 15% body fat, for someone who is 86 kilograms this means they have 12.9 kilograms of body fat. They can then make a clear decision of how many kilograms of body fat they want to lose.

But that's only one side of body composition. If you are 20% body fat, then what are you 80% of? Let's look at that next.

LEAN MASS

The other side of body fat percentage is known as your lean mass. The method established by Archimedes some 2,000 years ago is known as the two-compartment model. Just like Archimedes assumed the crown was made of two metals. we split the human body into two compartments: fat mass and lean mass.

What makes up lean mass? This is mineral weight (bone mass), water weight (fluid) and muscle mass. To estimate more than two compartments requires expensive equipment and technical know-how. You could pay hundreds of pounds for a one-off DEXA scan, but that doesn't give you a way to monitor your training and nutrition weekly.

The changes we see in lean mass we assume to be from lean muscle growth (or loss). Mineral loss would be a lot slower and indicative of a greater problem. Fluctuations in fluid are unlikely to be more than 1% of total body mass. Fluid is in a constant state of flux, so this is eradicated by our trailing average anyway. We're happy with a two-compartment model being sensitive enough to measure the changes in fat mass and muscle mass weekly. This just leaves muscle mass.

Earlier, I said weight loss is often used as a proxy for fat loss. Now we are using lean mass as a proxy for muscle mass. Only because we can eliminate fluctuation in mineral and fluid mass. If lean mass increases, we assume muscle mass has increased. An increase in lean mass is a good thing. More muscle mass means greater strength.

Action Steps

1. Download the body composition calculator.

2. Estimate your body fat percentage, fat mass and lean mass.

Next, we will take a closer look at lean mass and what your genetic potential is.

MUSCLE MASS POTENTIAL

More muscle is better. More muscle means more strength. The stronger you are, the better you move. A lot of men get put off by this idea because they see bodybuilders who have gone beyond the 'natural' capabilities of the human body for muscle mass. To compare your natural potential with chemically enhanced athletes is comparing apples to oranges.

Your genetic muscular potential is known as the Fat-Free Mass Index (FFMI). It is the same index that is applied to body weight but with fat mass removed. Think 'Fat-Free Mass' instead of 'Body Mass'. Take away fat mass and instead use lean mass then you have a number that shows your level of muscularity relative to your stature. This will tell you if you have a good amount of muscle relative to your frame size. This time the higher the number the better. Within the FFMI there is a cut-off that divides natural bodybuilders and enhanced bodybuilders. Even natural bodybuilders give everything they've got to achieve maximum levels of muscularity and hit a genetic ceiling. As a recreational gym-goer you should not fear this level of muscularity. If it takes a lot of dedication, it certainly will not happen by accident, I can assure you.

$$\frac{Lean\ Mass\ (kg)_{max}}{Height(m)^2} = Fat\ Free\ Mass\ Index$$

The Quetelet index was created by Adolphe Quetelet, a Belgian mathematician who theorised that you could determine the health of a population by measuring the 'area density' of the people. This is done by calculating the density of those people as boxes. The denser squares were less healthy. This was truer in the 19th century where people weren't so well fed, and resistance training wasn't as widespread. The anthropology of the population could be explained much simpler. We more commonly refer to the Quetelet Index as BMI. BMI is still used today although it is taken with a grain of salt. It works for *Mr. Joe Average* but is easily thrown off by abnormally high muscle mass or abnormally low fat mass, as seen in various athletes. There are too many variables, so if one of the variables is abnormal it throws off the entire calculation. By looking at someone you can easily tell if they are one of these anomalies and if their BMI is likely to be skewed. A high BMI because of increased fat mass is more likely for most people hence why even given its notoriety BMI still correlates with markers of poor health[5]. An average FFMI is reported as 19 kg/m^2. A good FFMI is 22 kg/m^2, and a ceiling is 25 kg/m^2. This makes it easy to remember as this is the same recommended range as the BMI scale.

---

[5] Patel, A. V., Hildebrand, J. S., & Gapstur, S. M. (2014). Body mass index and all-cause mortality in a large prospective cohort of white and black U.S. Adults. *PloS one*, 9(10), e109153. https://doi.org/10.1371/journal.pone.0109153

There is an approximate ceiling on natural genetic

potential at 25 kg/m². This was established in a study

comparing 83 elite enhanced bodybuilders and 74 elite

natural bodybuilders[6]. A handful of natural bodybuilders

came close to 25 but none exceeded this limit.

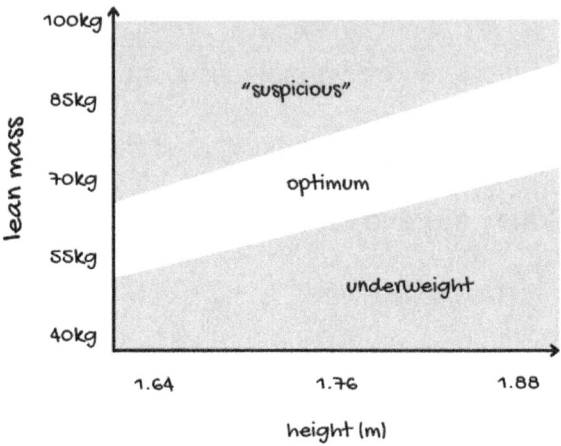

The next step is to reverse the formula assuming you

have a FFMI of 25 kg/m². By knowing your FFMI and your

height will tell you your maximum lean mass. Simply

multiply your height in metres squared by 25. For every

[6] Kouri, E. M., Pope, H. G., Jr, Katz, D. L., & Oliva, P. (1995). Fat-free mass index in users and nonusers of anabolic-androgenic steroids. *Clinical journal of sport medicine: official journal of the Canadian Academy of Sport Medicine*, 5(4), 223–228. https://doi.org/10.1097/00042752-199510000-00003

metre of height squared you have a maximum of 25 kg

of lean mass. Someone who is 6ft or 1.83 metres will

have a ceiling of 84 kilograms per m² of height. 1.83

squared equals 3.35. Multiplied by 25 equals 84

kilograms. This may sound confusing but it's relatively

simple when you look at the formula on the next page.

I'm 1.72 metres tall. If I square my height, 1.722 = 2.9584

then multiplying by 25 means I have a genetic ceiling of

73.96 kilograms of lean mass. It is highly unlikely that I

will get greater than this number.

$$If \; \frac{Lean\;Mass\;(kg)_{max}}{Height^2} = 25$$

$$Then \; 25 \times Height^2 = Lean\;Mass\;(kg)_{max}$$

With the advances in training and technology today

there may be a very small minority of men who can go

over 25 kg/m². Assuming you are not one of those, your

FFMI will be between 19 and 25. The goal is not to get to

25 but to shift towards it. Every unit that you shift up will

be a noticeable gain in muscularity. To put it into perspective an increase to your FFMI of 1 kg/m^2 will take an approximate addition of three kilograms, over six and a half pounds, of muscle mass. 25 kg/m^2 gives you the ceiling to aim towards. For example, for the average UK man who is 174cm tall his maximum lean mass is 25 x 1.74^2 = 75.7kg. The great thing is you only need to know your height. Height represents stature (frame size), you can calculate the maximum lean mass you can achieve with your height alone. Then you can estimate your total weight at an ideal body fat percentage. To estimate what your total weight should be at this maximum lean mass you just add either your current or your desired fat mass. Simply divide your lean mass percentage by your maximum lean mass. If you are currently 16% body fat and have a maximum lean mass of 75.5kg, divide 75.5 by 0.84 giving you a total weight of 89.9kg.

You can repeat the same process but this time with your desired body fat percentage. If he had a desired body fat percentage of 10% then 75.7kg would represent

90% of his total body weight. Divide 75.7 by 0.9, his total body mass at 10% body fat is 84.1kg.

This gives us a sensitive set of metrics that will help shape your goal setting. Instead of the oversimplified choice of whether to 'bulk' or 'cut,' consider the nuances of balancing body fat and lean mass. At different points in your training journey, you'll need to prioritize what will give you the biggest return for your efforts. Is that building muscle and strength or reducing fat and improving endurance. More on how to approach this trade-off will be covered in the nutrition and training sections.

Action Steps

1. Calculate your FFMI.
2. Calculate your maximum lean mass assuming a FFMI of 25
3. Calculate your total body mass at your maximum lean mass.
4. Calculate your ideal physique using your maximum lean mass and ideal body fat percentage.

Now you know where your fat mass and lean mass should be, Let's look at your proportions again. This time with a view to adding mass.

PROPORTIONS II

We've already discussed using your waist circumference as a marker of adiposity. After completing Proportions I, you should be making progress in reducing your body fat. This marks an exciting phase in your journey, as you can now shift your focus to developing the muscles that are beginning to emerge.

The statue of David in Florence, Italy is known around the world as a work of the great artist Michelangelo. But what if I told you that it wasn't Michelangelo that started the sculpture? Instead, the work was started at least 20 years before by Agostino Duccio and continued by Antonio Rossellino. The committee commissioning the artist wasn't happy with the earlier works. The proportions were poor. Michelangelo carried on the work and chiselled the sculpture to the Grecian ideal. The Grecian ideal states that there is a *golden ratio*. A number that appears in nature and is therefore most visually pleasing. The ratio is 1:1.618 and appears in art, architecture, design, and nature in trillions of places. The ratio itself is derived from the rate at which animals will theoretically replicate.

Many people may have heard of the golden ratio, but very few understand what it is based on. Leonardo Fibonacci wrote in his book *Liber Abaci* a thousand years ago the following sequence of numbers:

$$0, 1, 1, 2, 3, 5, 8, 13, 21, 34, 55, 89, 144 \dots$$

These numbers are based on a mathematical problem that if you left two rabbits alone, and it took the two rabbits one month to have another pair of rabbits, how many rabbits would you have after 12 months? The numbers in the sequence are the number of pairs of rabbits. After one month you would still have one pair of rabbits. Then they would double with the first offspring. Assuming they got straight back at it, it would take another month for the next pair of offspring, whilst the first offspring reached maturity. The rate of growth would accelerate. The rate at which the numbers accelerate, i.e., the difference between each number, is the golden ratio. As the numbers get larger the multiplier between subsequent numbers gets closer to the golden ratio of 1:1.618. 144/89 = 1.618. Although the above problem is a simplification to demonstrate the sequence of numbers. This sequence can be seen in the growth of microorganisms to the arrangement of seeds in a sunflower. When things are spaced according to the golden ratio it's because they grew according to the Fibonacci sequence.

The golden ratio of 1:1.618 has been used in art, architecture and more ever since. The godfather of bodybuilding in the 19th century Eugene Sandow - who has the Mr. Olympia trophy named after him - was the first to apply the golden ratio to bodybuilding. Sandow visited Italy when he was a young man and measured the renaissance statues. He found the golden ratio and calculated more proportions of the most pleasing male physiques. Early bodybuilders aimed to get as close to these perfectly proportioned physiques as possible. Before it became about the largest out of proportion muscle for the lowest possible body fat. And whilst the more recent greats would still pursue symmetry, they have lost sight of overall proportion.

The golden ratio can be seen in the waist to shoulder ratio to create an inverted cone shape with wide shoulders and a narrow waist. Once you have a waist that is approximately half your height, your shoulder circumference - measured around the outside of your upper body at the widest part of your shoulders - should be 1.618 times the circumference of your waist. This also means that your shoulder circumference should be 0.809 times your height.

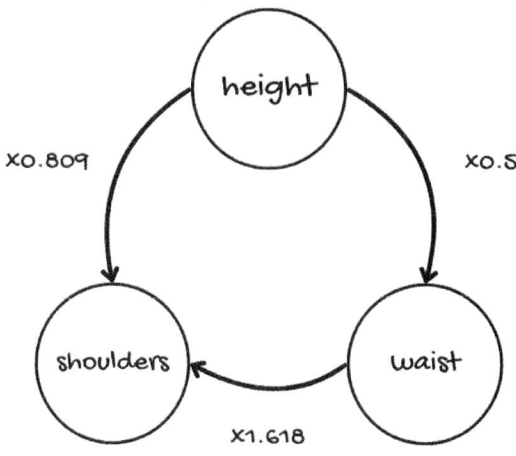

The golden ratio creates the most aesthetically pleasing dimensions, even the spacing of the features of the 'perfect' face. t seems logical that the first proportion you would strive for is an upper body that is 1.618 times the width of your midsection. As with a lot of what we have already discussed; if you don't necessarily achieve these proportions, but you are able to move somewhat closer towards them you will make a very noticeable difference to your physique. Larger chest and shoulders, larger thighs and smaller waists but maintaining proportion.

Previously we calculated your maximum lean mass as relative to your overall frame. We did this by using your height. We will continue to use your skeleton as a guide for how much muscle you can build. A larger the frame to hang the muscles upon the larger those muscles can be. As we go a level deeper, we are going to continue to use your bone structure as a reference for your muscle mass potential. We're now going to use the circumference of your wrists and ankles. Dr. Casey Butt has spent decades studying the genetic potential of bodybuilders. He found larger wrist and ankle circumferences meant larger lean muscle mass potential similarly to how we previously calculated FFMI. Dr. Butt also has a formula for calculating maximum muscular potential just like we did using the Fat-Free Mass Index. This formula instead uses wrist and ankle circumference.

To measure your wrist circumference, wrap a tape measure around your non-dominant wrist in the gap between the bony part of your wrist and your hand. This should be the narrowest part of your wrist. To measure your ankle, repeat the process, finding the narrowest point a few inches above your ankle. All measurements are in centimetres.

$$Lean\ Mass\ (kg)_{max}$$

$$= Height\ (cm)$$

$$\times \left(\frac{Wrist\ (cm)}{18.427} + \frac{Ankle\ (cm)}{15.182} \right)$$

$$\times \left(\frac{BF\%}{450} + 1 \right) \times 0.17863$$

Using Dr. Butt's formula gives you the same FFMI as using height squared. Measuring your wrists and ankles also give a good reference to your bone structure as the wrists and ankles have very little muscle mass or fat mass. A larger circumference means greater bone structure. Small frames have a very limited area for muscle attachment. Larger frames have more space for muscle attachment and are stronger and sturdier anchors and can support thicker, stronger muscles.

I found that Dr. Butt's formula gave the same FFMI as the height squared model. I use the height squared model but showing you this model leads nicely into Dr.

Butt's other research into finding the ideal proportions of segments of the male physique.

Dr. Butt has over his career had access to some of the greatest natural and enhanced bodybuilders and provides probably the most comprehensive reference available. Using your wrist and ankle circumferences, and Dr. Butt's equations, you can estimate the ideal proportions of areas of the body such as the thighs, calves, chest, and arms. The formula applies a multiplier to your wrist circumference for estimating your upper body proportions and your ankle circumference for your lower body proportions. Another multiplier is used that includes your body fat percentage. Higher body fat percentage is correlated with higher lean mass. This may seem counterintuitive to you, but as fat mass is accumulated by a spilling over of calorie intake, those who are athletic and have a higher fat mass also aren't short of lean mass too. Just think of strongmen, sumo wrestlers and rugby front row forwards. Each additional body fat percentage point adds about a quarter to a third

THE INTELLIGENT GUIDE TO FAT LOSS AND MUSCLE

of a percent to your muscular potential, so it makes a small but not insignificant difference.

Taking your wrist circumference, we can now calculate the maximum potential of your chest and your biceps.

$$Chest = 6.3138 \times Wrist\ (cm) \times \left(\frac{BF\%}{340} + 1\right)$$

$$Biceps = 2.3008 \times Wrist\ (cm) \times \left(\frac{BF\%}{265} + 1\right)$$

Taking your ankle circumference, we can now calculate the maximum potential of your thighs and your calves.

$$Thighs = 2.6785 \times Ankle\ (cm) \times \left(\frac{BF\%}{190} + 1\right)$$

$$Calves = 1.7780 \times Ankle\ (cm) \times \left(\frac{BF\%}{210} + 1\right)$$

These above formulae are intended, similarly, to the FFMI from the previous chapter, to show you what your genetic ceiling is. This is to show you what is possible with the correct nutrition and training. Which you will receive in the next two sections. It also takes a few years of consistent effort. I don't say this to put you off but to give you some perspective. The findings by Dr. Casey Butt were made by studying elite and drug-free bodybuilders. A bodybuilding off season where lean mass gains are achieved will take 1-2 years from a high starting point. If you are not starting from the same starting point, then expect your results to be a bit slower. Take your current chest, bicep, thigh and calf measurements. Subtract them from your genetic potential and break these down into several steps. Set a goal to achieve these over 6–12-month periods. Getting 20-30% towards your potential is a big and noticeable step.

These above calculations are the absolute genetic limit that you should be able to achieve naturally. Even to achieve 90% of this would put you in the top 1% of gym goers. (You can calculate 90% of these by calculating the difference between where you are now, where the above formulae put you and multiplying by 0.9).

Take me for example; I have 16.5cm wrists and 22cm ankles therefore the maximum circumferences are as follows:

- Chest: 108cm (currently 99cm)

- Biceps: 40cm (currently 36cm)

- Thighs: 63cm (currently 52cm)

- Calves: 41.5cm (currently 38cm)

I am only at 90% of my full potential (thighs are lagging somewhat) and therefore if I can add a couple of points to my FFMI I will likely see this gap close a little.

Action Steps

1. Calculate your genetic potential for your shoulders, chest, biceps, thighs, and calves.

Next, let's look at what you can do with the raw data as well as your body fat percentage.

FRIED EGG DIAGRAM

As mentioned earlier I don't tend to use bioelectrical impedance (BI) scales; the scales you step on the electrodes, and it estimates your body fat percentage. BI scales give a read-out without showing their working. Even if they did show you what it was measuring, resistance in ohms, there is no way of using this data effectively.

BI machines measure resistance and reactance of an electrical current. Now that you are taking circumference and skinfold measurements, you can picture the effectiveness of your body composition training. Think of a section of the body as if a cut has been made horizontally through the limb or trunk. You are measuring the circumference of the limb, the distance measured around the outside, and the thickness of the outermost layer, the adipose layer. If the fat mass and lean mass of our limbs were perfect concentric circles, we could use some basic maths to calculate the area of each segment. But they're not, how these two factors change in relation to each other tells us all we need to know. If the circumference of the limb is increasing, then you assume you are building muscle mass. If the skinfold thickness is decreasing, then you know that the adipose layer is shrinking.

Let's take the thigh for example. If you cut across the thigh, you will have a few rings. The thigh has a large volume of muscle mass made up primarily by the quadriceps, hamstrings, and adductors (not pictured), as well as other smaller muscles.

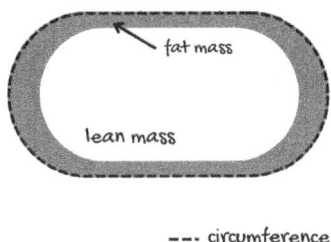

--- circumference

Effective resistance training using the legs will increase the size of these muscles. You also have the femur, the longest bone in the body but the mass of which will remain significantly unchanged. Between the muscle mass and the skin, you have the adipose layer which is spread relatively evenly around the entire circumference of the upper leg. You measure this layer of fat and skin by taking a thigh skinfold measurement.

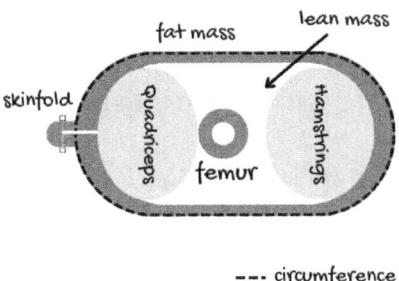

--- circumference

The fold is taken of the skin and the adipose layer together and the adipose is measured through the skin.

By taking a circumference measurement you are measuring the circumference of everything. An increase of either fat mass or lean mass will be seen as an increase in circumference measurement. This can be pictured like a fried egg with the lean mass represented by the yolk of the egg and the fat mass being represented by the egg white. The combination of measurements is more useful than each individual measures alone. Whilst it might be quicker and easier to step on some BI scales, I would rather get specific measurements that I can view objectively. If I want to increase the circumference of my thighs, I can change the volume of my training and keep measuring. My results won't get lost in a single overall measure. If my lean mass is increasing and my thigh circumference is as well, I know my training is working. The goal is to increase the circumference of the limbs and chest, as they have a larger muscle mass. Decreasing the skinfold measurement will tell you that you are losing fat overall.

Next, if you imagine the abdomen, which has a lot less muscle mass but greater fat mass. You will take the same measurements, but the results will have different meanings. You are looking to reduce the circumference of your abdomen and reduce the skinfold measurement. Abdominal skinfold correlates pretty closely to overall body fat percentage. Being able to see the abdominal muscles beneath the abdominal is entirely dependent on the skinfold thickness of the abdomen. Having visible abs or a six-pack is not a birth right. Everyone can have a six-pack if they reduce their abdominal skinfold to approximately 10mm. The average man in my experience who starts my program has an abdominal skinfold of around 30mm. Consistently losing 1mm per week from the abdominal skinfold will take 20 weeks to achieve a defined abdomen. Given that most men training alone will give up within six to twelve weeks will tell you why six-packs are seen as the holy grail. It's not impossible to achieve, it just takes more consistency.

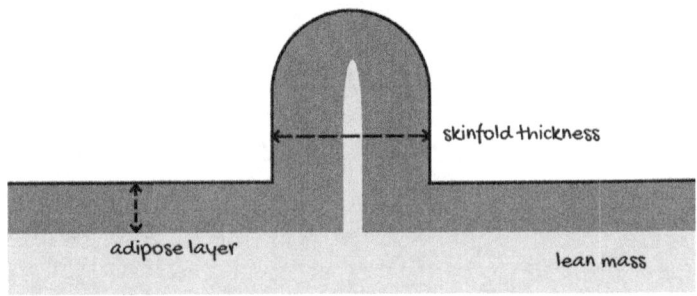

skinfold thickness

adipose layer

lean mass

There are no action steps in this section. Hopefully I have helped you visualise the transformation you are trying to achieve. You are trying to reduce fat mass measured through the skinfold and increase the lean mass through the overall circumference of your limbs.

Finally, let's look at how you track your fat mass and lean mass changes each week.

PROTEIN RATIO

I am going to finish this section by talking about how you can monitor the quality of your fat loss without taking any more measurements. As you are already tracking weight, and body composition, you can use these two metrics to score your fat loss each week. This is by using the protein ratio or p-ratio for short. The p-ratio represents the weekly changes in lean mass proportional to changes in total body weight.

The p-ratio tells you how much of your weight loss (or gain) is lean mass. The less lean mass you lose the better. This is expressed like this:

$$\frac{Changes\ in\ Lean\ Mass\ (kg)}{Changes\ in\ Body\ Mass\ (kg)} = P - Ratio$$

This is shown as the percentage of weight change that is lean mass. If you lose one kilogram of total body mass and half of this weight loss is lean mass then you have a p ratio of 0.5, or 50%. There are changes you can make to improve your p-ratio that will be discussed later.

There is no exact number to aim for, but, if your goal is fat loss, an ideal p ratio is one that is as small as possible. If your goal is to gain muscle, then an ideal p-ratio is one that is as high as possible. If you were to lose all fat mass then you have a p-ratio of 0, this means you have lost 100% fat and 0% lean mass. If you gained total body mass and all of it was muscle then you have a p-ratio of 1, you have gained 100% muscle and 0% fat mass. Typically, the p-ratio is somewhere between these two extremes. The human body is never 100% efficient so it's unlikely that all weight loss is fat loss, or all weight gain is muscle gain. The change in weight that you see is the net change of a lot of separate processes. Fat metabolism and muscle protein synthesis are two of these separate processes. Fat metabolism requires an energy deficit to start the process of turning stored energy into mechanical energy. Muscle protein synthesis requires a stimulus and adequate protein and energy to produce new muscle tissue.

There are a few scenarios that exploit the above rules, where the p-ratio can be either less than 0, or greater than 1. A p-ratio of less than 0 means that you have lost more lean mass than total weight, say if you lost one kilogram of overall weight and two kilograms of lean mass. This would be a state of atrophy or detraining, sometimes seen when injured and immobilised and unable to train.

If your total body weight decreases but you increase lean mass, you will have a p-ratio greater than 1. This is not uncommon in novices or people returning to training after a break. This reflects a 'bounce-back' effect where fluid and nutrient levels inside and outside of muscle tissue are returning to normal. The p-ratio will likely fall back within the normal range of 0 to 1 in a matter of weeks.

The p-ratio is an observation of what has occurred. It is just like body fat percentage in that it is entirely conceptual. It only exists in a spreadsheet or on a piece of paper, nowhere else. But it is a useful tool to judge your progress each week. There is no ideal p-ratio. Higher in muscle gain and lower in fat loss is all you can aim for. you will have to find your p-ratio and monitor it over the weeks you are training and take small steps to improve it. Going over hundreds of my past client data I found p-ratios that ranged from 0.04 to 0.66, but the average p-ratio was 0.25. For every kilogram of total body weight lost, a quarter of it was lean mass and three quarters of it was fat mass.

A note of caution, there are no perfect measurements, only good-enough estimations. You are taking one theoretical number from a calculation, to create another calculation. Any noise or error that is created in estimating body composition will have a knock-on effect on the p-ratio. Use the p-ratio as a general indicator of the speed and efficiency that you are losing fat mass. If your p-ratio is consistently high, then you can take steps to reduce it. Likewise, if your p-ratio is consistently low when you are aiming to gain lean mass then it's an indicator that you're trying to gain weight too quickly.

To improve a p-ratio you must improve fat metabolism and muscle protein synthesis. You can improve both, but they are independent systems, they both rely on some of the same things often in conflicting environments. This is where the belief that you can't build muscle and burn fat at the same time. You can. However, you cannot build *optimal* muscle and burn *optimal* fat at the same time. You have a trade-off to create an environment where moderate fat loss and muscle gain can be created. As you progress you will be attempting to achieve more marginal gains. You must better suit your environment to one condition at the expense of the other. Simultaneous fat loss and muscle gain gets harder. This is why bodybuilders have separate bulking and cutting phases where they optimise one environment at the expense of the other. They try to maintain the gains achieved in one phase through the other. Novice trainers have such large margins of error, at the opposite end to marginal gains, these environments will overlap. Simultaneous muscle gain and fat loss can occur. These overlapping margins will shrink over time until two very separate environments are required. A decision about training priorities must be made. When to prioritise muscle gain over fat loss as vice versa.

Now that you have finished the measurements section you are able to take your weight, skinfolds of your chest, abdominal and thigh, circumferences of your neck, wrist, forearm, chest, waist, and hip. You can put these ten measurements into estimations for body fat percentage, lean mass, fat mass, free fat mass index, p-ratio and ideal proportions for your waist, chest, bicep, thigh, and calf. For only a handful of measurements you can now paint a vivid picture of your body composition. Now let's turn your attention to the steps to optimise fat loss and muscle building in the next two sections.

First, we'll look at how quality nutrition is key to losing fat mass and gaining muscle mass.

SECTION 2 - NUTRITION

Nutrition is arguably the most important aspect of a healthy program. Training sends a stimulus for change., even a poor training plan will. Whether or not that change occurs depends largely on your nutrition. You can train the best you ever have but if you are still overeating you will still accumulate fat mass. Likewise, if your nutrition is poor, you will unlikely grow new muscle mass. Use the p-ratio as your guiding principle to highlight the two changes you are trying to make. Neither fat mass loss nor muscle mass gain are achievable without sound nutrition. Fat is only burned if the equivalent deficit in the nutrition is present. You cannot build new muscle tissue if you are not consuming protein to provide the necessary building blocks.

In this section we are going to look at the quality of your nutrition, how and why your body stores fat, how we can give your body everything it needs to build muscle and more importantly to stay healthy and improve your quality of life.

Let's first look at the quality of your nutrition.

FOOD QUALITY

We are coming round to the idea that food is more than just the sum of its ingredients, and this is often a sentiment that is lost on those that are tracking calories or macros. They forget the interaction of the hundreds of different foods that we eat per week and where they come from. That said, you would probably agree with me if I said the quality of food plays as much a role as the quantity of food.

Food processing is incredibly important, without it we'd be forced to eat the food that is grown or reared within a few miles of where we lived. If we had a typically bad year for crops people would die. With processing we can now share food around the globe, giving us access to exotic, fresh foods all year round. Food processing made huge leaps during the two world wars. Canning and freeze-drying were methods invented to send food to troops on front lines all around the world. However, ultra-processed foods are becoming more popular now more than ever. Ultra-processed ingredients are appearing in all types of food. Food processing is now used to change the flavour, texture, palatability, and digestibility of food to make us consume more and more. A loaf of bread should contain four ingredients: flour, water, yeast, and salt. However, look on the ingredients list of your supermarket bread and it's not uncommon for it to contain fifteen or more ingredients. The same five ingredients to make the bread and another ten to fifteen to make it easier to ship and store. Whilst we don't fully understand the full extent to which ultra-processed foods affect our health. We do know those that eat more ultra-processed foods are worse off health wise. People who consume more ultra-processed foods are at greater risk of cardiovascular disease, type 2 diabetes, anxiety, depression, sleep disorders and obesity[7].

There are several classification systems for processed foods. One is called the NOVA system (Portuguese: 'new system') which classifies foods into one of four groups. Group one contains all the foods that are derived from the edible parts of plants and animals that haven't been processed. These are the foods you will buy in the fresh food sections of the supermarket, or your grandparents would have bought from the butcher and greengrocer. Group two classifies all the cooking ingredients derived from group one that are used in the normal cooking process. These are the things you will have at home and use when cooking, such as dairy produce, butter, oils, salt etc. Group three contains processed foods from combining group one ingredients with group two

---

[7] Lane, M. M., Gamage, E., Du, S., Ashtree, D. N., McGuinness, A. J., Gauci, S., Baker, P., Lawrence, M., Rebholz, C. M., Srour, B., Touvier, M., Jacka, F. N., O'Neil, A., Segasby, T., & Marx, W. (2024). Ultra-processed food exposure and adverse health outcomes: umbrella review of epidemiological meta-analyses. BMJ (Clinical research ed.), 384, e077310. https://doi.org/10.1136/bmj-2023-077310

ingredients such as freshly baked bread, canned vegetables, and cured meats. Finally, group four foods are industrially processed foods that have little if any group one derivatives such as sweets and snacks that have little to no recognisable food ingredients. Confusing? Yes, and you're not alone. If you struggle to get your head around the difference of the four groups, even professional dietitians struggle with the classifications[8]. A group of twenty dieticians could only agree on 30% of over 200 hundred foods that were either packaged as healthy, or were common unpackaged foods such as fruit, vegetables, meats, cheese, and yoghurt. We're not talking about getting a few of group two and three mixed up, the dieticians were putting some foods at the entirely wrong end. In fact, yoghurt was one of a few foods that was split evenly across the four groups by the dietitians. Likewise, most dietitians put

---

[8] Braesco, V., Souchon, I., Sauvant, P., Haurogné, T., Maillot, M., Féart, C., & Darmon, N. (2022). Ultra-processed foods: how functional is the NOVA system?. European journal of clinical nutrition, 76(9), 1245–1253. https://doi.org/10.1038/s41430-022-01099-1

orange juice in group four even though group one included "fresh, squeezed, chilled, frozen, or dried fruits." This isn't to demonstrate the lack of understanding by the dietitians. These are the group of people who are most knowledgeable when it comes to understanding the health of foods. Instead, this shows that it's not possible to split foods into neat exclusive groups.

Rather than four exclusive groups, processed and ultra-processed foods should be seen as a sliding scale. From one end of the scale, you have edible animal and plant parts that have had no processing to industrially processed substances at the other end. You don't have to be a dietitian to understand how to improve the quality of your food choices. Choose more foods from the left of the scale where foods are as close to their raw state as possible and fewer choices from the right of the scale where food is industrially processed into shapes where the original foods aren't easily discernible. You don't have to become a 'clean eating' advocate overnight. Shifting your position more leftwards, less processed, along this scale will have noticeable effects on your health. Ultra-processed foods are easy to spot because they will contain a long list of ingredients that aren't part of preparing the food, instead they are there to make it easier for the producer to ship or store it. Take some popular household crisps in the UK. One brand has three ingredients: potato (NOVA1), salt (NOVA2) and vegetable oil (NOVA2). Compare it to another popular brand which contains nine ingredients, none of which are NOVA1, five are from NOVA2 and the remaining four are ultra-processed ingredients (NOVA4). The lesson here is not to become anal about the ingredients when choosing crisps. I have used crisps as an example. I could have chosen any number of foods where what we understand the food to be is replaced by dozens of ingredients that will imitate what the food is supposed to be. This is a telling story of how our food is resembling food less and less. A few good rules of thumb are: if you recognise the ingredients in the ingredients list as things you would keep in your kitchen cupboards, would your grandmother have used them in her cooking, or could you explain what they are to a six-year-old? I highly recommend reading *Food Rules* by Michael Pollan for lot's more food rules that are easy to follow without having to count calories (yet).

The key is not to have hard-and-fast rules to eliminate processed foods, but instead to have fewer of them and more unprocessed foods. I'm not a fan of restricting diets and telling you what you cannot have. The goal here is to fill your meals with fresh fruits, vegetables, meat, and fish then you will leave less room for the foods you should be having less of. The last thing I want you to get bogged down with, especially in the early days of your journey, is whether food A is better than food B.

Unprocessed foods give you more nutrients for your calories and fewer calories for the volume of food you eat. This makes you feel fuller and means you can eat more. The secret to a successful diet is eating more but still getting great results. For example, let's take a popular bag of kids' sweets (grown-ups love them too).

The bag is 160 grams, if like me, you have been known to eat an entire bag by yourself on a car journey then you would have eaten nearly 550 kilocalories of energy. That's enough energy to run approximately 6 miles. The food that you have eaten to get that energy only weighs 160 grams and takes up a volume of only a couple of hundred millilitres. Probably less space than a soda can. However, for the same amount of energy you could eat 48 satsumas. Which would weigh a total of 3.6 kilograms and take up as much space as 25 soda cans. But still giving you the same 550 kilocalories of energy. You're probably unlikely to be able to eat 48 satsumas. If you ate two satsumas instead of half a bag of sweets, you're saving over 100 kilocalories. You're going to feel a lot fuller having eaten double the weight and over four times the volume of food. These foods have their place, I'm not for banning them entirely. If you are running a half marathon a pocket full of sweets comes in handy, it saves you from having to eat a satsuma every quarter of a mile! Apply this to all your foods and you will see that unprocessed foods are less energy dense, contain more micronutrients and fibre, and will take up more space in your gut. This is how you eat more food but lose more weight. You eat a greater volume of food yet save hundreds of calories.

In the following chapters I'm going to teach you how to structure a diet based on macronutrients. First, it's important to get the right overall picture of your diet. Start to keep a food log of everything you eat. Then take what you have learned in this and score the foods in your food log. We're not going to use the NOVA system because the difference between groups is too ambiguous. In fact, we're not going to worry about the food in the middle at all because this isn't where the biggest difference is to be made. Count the minimally processed foods and the ultra-processed foods.

Most of your diet should come from unprocessed foods from animal and plant sources. Your plate should have a source of protein, this will cover your protein and in some cases fat requirements. You should then have plenty of vegetables or fruit for your carbohydrates and micronutrients. Finally add some grains if needed to complete your carbohydrates. Base your square meals around the above formula. Then on top of your square meals, allow a small proportion, 10-20% of your calories, or one or two snacks a day where you don't worry about the quality as such. We know our bodies can handle some in moderation, so you don't have to exclude them fully from your diet. In fact, a little bit can go a long way psychologically in making your diet more sustainable.

Find a handful of meals that you are confident in preparing and that you enjoy and build your repertoire around these. At the end of the chapter, I give you an example of what a day might look like, but it's important that you have your own repertoire that you can follow. Only a registered dietician can prescribe a meal plan. I can give you the overall structure and give you recommendations. It is your responsibility to follow these guidelines and adapt your diet plan to suit your individual circumstances.

There are other strategies you can take to make your nutrition simple and sustainable. Have some staples that you can rely on and make some simple 'go-to' meals if you're ever in doubt. Search online for recipes; some websites let you search by ingredient. Search for recipes with keywords such as 'vegetable' or chicken breast'.

It is important to build a foundation of quality foods before you look at calories and macronutrients. Having control over the ingredients will help later when you need to adjust the ingredients to adjust the levels of your macronutrients. Not enough protein, fibre, and micronutrients and too much fat and simple carbohydrates is usually the issue of a current diet. If your dinners are from ready meals, there is little if anything that you can do to adjust the macronutrient levels. If you are making the meals from scratch, you can adjust the quantities of the ingredients to change the macronutrient profile. Including adding more vegetables to increase the volume of foods whilst hardly changing the calories. This is an important point I don't want you to miss before we

move on to the details of your diet.

	Spaghetti Bolognese 'Ready Meal'	Homemade Spaghetti Bolognese
Calories	532 kcal	684 kcal
Fat	17g	22g
Carbohydrate	64g	70g
Protein	27g	50g
Weight	400g	750g
Energy Density	1.33 kcal/g	0.91 kcal/g

Look at the above comparison. An 'if-it-fits-your-

macros' approach, where you judge foods solely on their

macronutrient composition, would tell you that a

homemade bolognese is worse than a microwave ready-

meal. But if I'm making a bolognese myself I'm using

wholewheat pasta for a glycaemic index 20% lower and

400% more fibre than white pasta. I have doubled the

protein content and I'm meeting all my micronutrient

needs by adding two tins of chopped tomatoes, a whole

white onion, a pepper, a courgette, two sticks of celery, a carrot, a clove of garlic, a handful of spinach and half a handful of basil leaves. The ready meal has onion, mushroom and carrot and is bulked out with wheat flour and corn flour. I use a 600g pack of lean beef mince for four servings, compared to the 75g of beef of unknown quality in the ready meal. It should come as no surprise that my homemade meal above is twice the volume than a small ready meal and therefore will leave you much fuller for longer.

In the chapters that follow I am going to go into much more detail on protein, carbohydrates, and fats. But the lesson here should now be clear that food quality is just as important. You need to take the quality of the food you eat as your top priority. The food manufacturers prioritise making foods easy to ship and store and manufacturing them in a way that makes you, the consumer, consume more.

Action Steps

1. Keep a food log of everything you eat.

2. Count the total 'minimally processed foods' and 'ultra-processed foods'.

3. Create a repertoire of healthy go-to meals using minimally processed foods.

Next, we'll start to look at the calories in your diet and work out a budget together.

ENERGY

The average man has enough energy in his fat stores to run approximately 50 marathons. Fat cells are energy stores for the excess energy consumed in the diet. To reduce those energy stores you must burn an excess of energy. Everything you eat and drink except for water contains energy. You store all the energy that you consume, that energy either gets used or stored long term.

From the previous section you have estimated how much body fat you have and how much body fat you want to have. From this we can estimate how much energy you have stored within that excess body fat. A kilogram of body fat contains 7,700 kilocalories of energy. To reduce your body fat to a desired level you can calculate approximately how much energy over time you will need to burn. Multiply the kilograms of fat you want to lose by the number of kilocalories in one kilogram.

If you are 86 kilograms, 20% body fat and your goal is 10% body fat then your goal is to lose 8.6 kilograms. You will have to burn 66,220 kcal of energy, 7,700 kcal for each of the 8.6 kilograms of body fat. If you remember from the p-ratio chapter, it is likely that you will be losing approximately 75% fat and 25% lean mass. An eight-kilogram fat loss will require approximately a twelve-kilogram weight loss. As you are tracking body composition you just need to remember that you will be tracking fat loss as well as weight loss. You keep going until you achieve your fat loss goal.

The goal of this chapter is to help you figure out what a realistic timeframe is to achieve your goal. Also, what adjustments to make if things aren't going according to plan. As we have established in the previous chapter, food is more than the energy it provides however all food contains energy. Realistically, you cannot change the amount of body fat you have stored in your body without adjusting your energy intake. Your energy intake will be dictated by how much energy you burn. The difference between your energy intake and your energy expenditure will determine what changes occur. Your expenditure may fluctuate from day to day, but I recommend taking an average, unless you have certain days that are very different to the norm.

Firstly, you need to take a baseline estimate of your metabolism. Just like in the previous section you will use predictive statistics to estimate your metabolism. As a side note, metabolism just means the sum of all the anabolic (building) and catabolic (breaking-down) reactions in your body. Resting Energy Expenditure (REE) or Basal Metabolic Rate (BMR) are used interchangeably as indicators of how much energy you burn per day idling i.e., at rest. BMR and REE technically mean slightly different things so from here on out we will use REE.

The most accurate way to directly measure REE is by sleeping overnight at a laboratory and having your expired air taken from a mask. The difference between the atmospheric air and the air you are exhaling will tell the experimenters how much energy you are burning whilst resting. This is known as direct calorimetry. The expired air is analysed as a product of the reactions that are occurring in your body as energy is released from energy stores. The more carbon dioxide, the more energy has been used. This is not practical for us, so there are some simple equations that have been compared to direct calorimetry that can get us close enough. These use body weight, lean mass, height, and age to predict REE.

Using Weight only

Owen Formula

$$REE = 10.2 \times Weight\ (kg) + 879$$

Shoefield Formula

$$REE = 11.472 \times Weight\ (kg) + 873.1$$

Tinsley Formula

$$REE = 24.8 \times Weight\ (kg) + 10$$

Using Lean Mass only

Mifflin St. Jeor Formula

$$REE = 19.7 \times Lean\ Mass\ (kg) + 413$$

Cunningham Formula

$$REE = 21.6 \times Lean\ Mass\ (kg) + 370$$

Tinsley Formula

$$REE = 25.9 \times Lean\ Mass\ (kg) + 284$$

Cunningham Formula

$$REE = 22 \times Lean\ Mass\ (kg) + 500$$

Using Weight, Height and Age

De Lorenzo Formula

$$REE = 9 \times Weight\ (kg) + 11.7 \times Height\ (cm) - 857$$

Harris-Benedict Formula

$$REE = 13.75 \times Weight\ (kg) + 5 \times Height\ (cm)$$
$$- 6.76 \times Age\ (years) + 66.47$$

Mifflin St. Jeor Formula

$$REE = 9.99 \times Weight \ (kg) + 6.25 \times Height \ (cm)$$

$$- \ 4.92 \times Age \ (years) + 5$$

Roza-Shigal Formula

$$REE = 13.397 \times Weight \ (kg) + 4.799 \times Height \ (cm)$$

$$- \ 5.677 \times Age \ (years) + 88.362$$

Bernstein Formula

$$REE = 11.02 \times Weight \ (kg) + 10.23 \times Height \ (cm)$$

$$- \ 5.8 \times Age \ (years) - 1032$$

All the above formulae will predict your resting energy expenditure, with slightly varying accuracy. They can all over- or under- estimate for different people. They use combinations of weight, lean mass, height, and age to paint a picture of, and estimate your resting energy expenditure.

Let's take a 95kg man, who is 180cm tall and 40 years old, he also has 66 kg of lean mass. According to the Owen Formula (weight only) his REE is 1,848 kcal per day. According to the Mifflin St. Jeor Formula (lean mass only) his REE is 1,720 kcal per day. The De Lorenzo Formula (weight and height) puts his REE at 1,723 kcal per day. Finally, the Roza-Shigal Formula (weight, height, and age) puts his REE at 1,998 kcal per day. As you can see there is quite a bit of variance between the three, but we can take an average of 1,822 kcal per day. I take the average of all twelve formulae. I'd rather a strong average in the middle of everyone than counting exclusively on one formula.

As weight, lean mass and height increase so too does resting energy expenditure. As age increases resting energy expenditure decreases. You'd imagine a heavier, leaner, taller and younger person to burn more energy when resting. This is only your baseline metabolism and is a starting point. The biggest factor, and a multiplier of, how much energy you burn per day is how active you are. Your activity level multiplies your resting energy expenditure. The energy you burn is dialled up the more vigorously you move. The more you move your body, the more energy is required to fuel this movement. Whilst your age, height, and weight (at any moment) are out of your control, how much you move day-to-day is very much within your control.

Someone who doesn't exercise and has a sedentary job will only burn 20% more than their resting energy expenditure per day. A moderately active person will burn 55% more energy than at rest and someone who is extremely active, such as an athlete or a labourer, can double their energy expenditure.

Here are the average activity levels that typically get used:

Activity Level	Multiplier
Sedentary	1.2
Light Active	1.375
Moderately Active	1.55
Active	1.725
Very Active	1.9

When you multiply your REE by your activity level you get your total daily energy expenditure (TDEE). I take an average and it's about right. My REE is approximately 1,700 kcal per day. I am moderately active, so my TDEE is in the region of 2,600 kcal per day. This makes sense with observations I make when tracking my diet. I do have days that are more active where I will burn at or above 3,000 kcal per day. An average of 3,000 kcal per day is the tipping point where I start to gain weight gradually. On the flip side, my weight will start to drop if I start eating consistently below 2,500 kcal per day.

The best way to find out how much energy you burn per day is to monitor your calorie intake and note any changes in your weight over a week or more. If your weight stays the same over a week then the calories, you have consumed are also the calories you have burned. As a note of caution, the average man in the UK will underestimate calorie intake by up to 50%[9]. The easiest way to track your calorie intake is via an app. Don't leave anything out! As a minimum I'd monitor at the very least

---

[9] Government Statistical Service. (2016, August 8). *A Government Statistical Service perspective on official estimates of calorie consumption*. Office for National Statistics. Retrieved from https://www.ons.gov.uk

two weekdays and one weekend day and observe the change in my weight after a week.

Go to https://intelligentshedder.com/tools and download the nutrition plan. Calculate your REE and approximate your activity level. This will give you your total daily energy expenditure.

Remember, fat cells are predominantly long-term energy stores. So fat tissue holds a certain amount of energy. As we established earlier, each kilogram of body fat stores approximately 7,700 kcal of energy. To calculate how much of a deficit you need, first take how many kilograms of body fat you wish to lose and multiply it by 7,700. This will give you the total energy deficit you will need to have to burn this amount of body fat. This is because if your diet is deficient by this amount of energy your body will refer to its energy stores for the exact difference.

A word of caution, don't go too extreme when setting your deficit goals and your timeframe. A rule of thumb, set your REE as a hard floor and do not go below your

REE for calorie intake per day. Although all food has a calorie value, by restricting food intake to reduce calorie intake, you also restrict vital nutrients. You can supplement with a daily multivitamin, but the best approach is to go with a moderate calorie deficit. Also, too extreme of a calorie deficit and your p-ratio will sky-rocket. Not only will you be losing body fat but you will be giving up vital lean mass too. Remember we are not pursuing weight loss at all costs. We are trying to strike an intelligent balance between maximum fat loss and minimum lean mass loss.

If we go back to the above example used to calculate REE; our 95-kilogram man. He has a REE of 1,822 kcal per day. He is currently sedentary so he typically will burn less than 2,200 kcal per day. He probably eats the usual 500-700 kcal meals every day. Snacking and drinking can add hundreds of calories per day, which easily adds up to excess of over 2,200 kcal and fat mass starts to slowly creep on. The good news is he's now focusing on his health and a big part of that is he's increasing his activity level. He now exercises three times per week and is generally more active. We're going to assume that he is now 40% more active than his baseline. This means he is now burning 2,550 kcal per day. As we know every kilogram of body fat that he wants to lose will take a surplus of activity of 7,700 kcal. As he is now burning a weekly total of 17,850 kcal he can lose one kilogram of fat in a week if he drops his calorie intake to 1,450 kcal per day. But this violates the rule of not dropping below REE. Instead, he sets a more realistic target of losing one kilogram every fourteen days. This means he will eat 2,000 kcal per day, giving him a deficit of 550 kcal from the 2,550 kcal he is now burning every day.

This is the smart way to set calorie targets. The healthy way is to handle your calorie intake like a budget. Don't expect to be perfect every single day, but at least you have a realistic plan to aim for and to get back should you slip up. You also have the methods above to intelligently monitor your weight and estimate your body composition. If you are not progressing the way you think you ought to be then you can make small adjustments each week.

The best way to monitor if this is working successfully, as we looked at earlier, is by using the T7D for your weight. If the numbers are falling steadily regardless of what is happening daily, then you know you're in a calorie deficit.

Gaining Muscle

When trying to gain new muscle mass the common belief is that you need an energy surplus because of the energy demands of creating new muscle tissue. As stated at the start of this chapter you already have enough energy in your body to run 50 marathons. There is enough energy to build muscle. So why do you need to be in a calorie surplus to gain muscle?

It's not a surplus of calories that you need *per se*, instead, you need to avoid an energy deficit. This ensures you have an adequate supply of resources particularly protein of which to build muscle from and carbohydrate to ensure insulin levels are maintained to shuttle nutrients into muscles. When vital nutrients are sparse the human body will try to protect itself and downregulate non-essential processes. Building additional muscle is a non-essential process. Your survival doesn't directly rely on you building muscle daily. Some studies have looked at bodybuilders during their final prep for a contest where they are trying to trim off as much fat as possible. They can be in an energy deficit for twenty weeks or more. The result of a prolonged energy deficit is that hormones including testosterone and thyroid hormones are significantly decreased[10]. Down regulating these hormones will limit muscle growth. In the final bodybuilding prep phase athletes will lose significant muscle. If they lose less muscle than they built during their off-season.

---

[10] Schoenfeld, B. J., Alto, A., Grgic, J., Tinsley, G., Haun, C. T., Campbell, B. I., Escalante, G., Sonmez, G. T., Cote, G., Francis, A., & Trexler, E. T. (2020). Alterations in Body Composition, Resting Metabolic Rate, Muscular Strength, and Eating Behavior in Response to Natural Bodybuilding Competition Preparation: A Case Study. Journal of strength and conditioning research, 34(11), 3124–3138. https://doi.org/10.1519/JSC.0000000000003816

The energy is already there. All you need to do to gain muscle from an energetics point of view is avoid a prolonged deficit. Combined with training well and recovering fully and you will grow muscle. It's a common misconception that to gain muscle you need to eat as much as possible. In a study by The Norwegian School of Sport Sciences, when a group of athletes increased their calories modestly, but did not count their calories, they gained only 1.5% increase in body weight compared to those given a specific weight gain diet plan. There was no difference between the two groups in the amount of lean mass they gained, but the intervention group gained five times more body fat[11]. Increasing energy intake far beyond maintenance will not increase the amount of muscle you gain. Instead, the excess energy will just have to be stored as excess body fat, defeating the object of trying to improve leanness. My advice if your goal is

---

[11] Garthe I, Raastad T, Refsnes PE, Sundgot-Borgen J. Effect of nutritional intervention on body composition and performance in elite athletes. Eur J Sport Sci. 2013;13(3):295-303. doi: 10.1080/17461391.2011.643923. Epub 2012 Mar 1. PMID: 23679146.

adding muscle mass is to start at maintenance calories, the number of calories required to maintain your current body weight, and then increase gradually from there.

Once you have your total daily energy intake goal you can split this further into the ideal number of meals per day. There is no significant difference in splitting a daily total into anything from three to six meals per day. The deciding factor will most likely be the size and the frequency of the meals. Splitting into smaller and more frequent meals is a personal choice. For example, if your daily energy intake goal is 2,000 kcal, splitting it into four meals per day will give you a target of 500 kcal. If you go over on one meal, you can use the other meals to make it up. We will apply this same logic with the following chapters.

Action Steps

1. Calculate your resting energy expenditure (REE)
2. Estimate your activity level (AL)

3. Calculate your total daily energy expenditure (TDEE)

4. Calculate your required energy deficit and your new calorie intake target.

Your body gets energy from the four macro- (large) -nutrients. These are protein, fat, carbohydrate, and alcohol. Let's look at macronutrients in general first.

MACRONUTRIENTS

There are four main nutrients that your body will process energy from: protein, carbohydrate, fat, and alcohol. These macronutrients are different arrangements of Hydrogen, Carbon, and Oxygen. Protein also contains Nitrogen. This makes protein, carbohydrate, fat, and alcohol organic compounds. Fats are chains of fatty acids, proteins are chains of amino acids and carbohydrates are chains of saccharides. The length and structure of each of these chains will determine the characteristics of the macronutrient they make up. Saturated fats have chains of fatty acids linked entirely by single bonds of carbon. Unsaturated fats have one or more double bonds that changes the structure and means the fat molecule isn't fully composed of single carbon bonds.

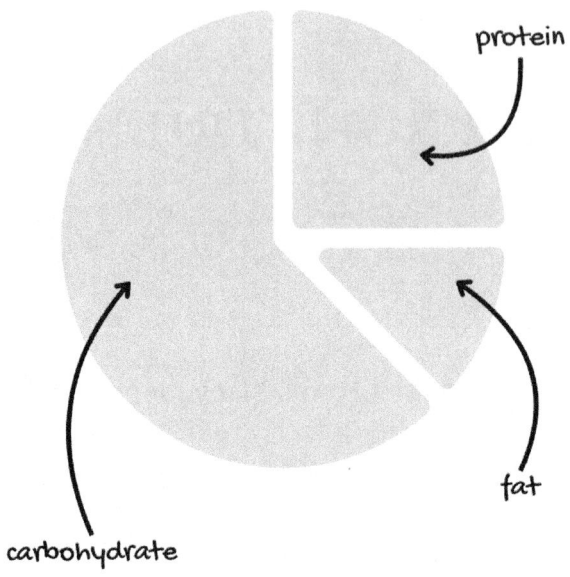

Just like we thought about the body as having two compartments, we can also think of food as having multiple compartments. Let's take an apple as an example; we have the two compartments, energy containing and non-energy containing compartments of the food. For an apple, by measuring the sum of the protein, carbohydrate, and fat we have the energy containing mass of the apple. Which for a 100g apple is 12g, that means that 88g of the mass of the apple doesn't provide any energy at all. This is largely made up of water but there will be some micronutrients and fibre as well. Of that 12 grams, all twelve grams are carbohydrates, with zero grams of fat or protein. The greater the energy providing compartment of an individual food the greater the energy density of the food. The energy density can simply be illustrated as the number of calories of energy that food provides per mass, typically 100g. Let's compare the apple with a cookie. To keep it simple I have just baked a perfect cookie of 100g to compare with the apple. This 100g cookie has 472 kilocalories of energy. Out of this 100g of cookie 90 grams provide energy; seven grams of protein, 60 grams of carbohydrate and 23 grams of fat. Only ten grams are non-energy-providing. This means the energy density of the cookie is 472 kilocalories per 100 grams. That is ten times the energy provided by the apple, or looking at it another way you could eat ten apples to provide the same amount of energy as one cookie. Ten apples would take up a lot more space in your stomach and be a lot harder to eat than a single cookie.

Using weight to describe food can be incredibly helpful but it means we can often overlook the volume of food. The volume is the amount of space that food occupies. If you consider dehydrated food. They have the exact same nutrient profile as their non-dried counterpart, but the water has been removed. When you rehydrate them, you decrease their density. This is useful for storing and transporting grains such as pasta and rice and some fruits. A lot of people get in trouble because their stomach is barely registering any contents, such as a cookie, the amount of energy it provides is huge.

Your stomach has a capacity of just under a litre and takes two to four hours to empty. How well you manage your weight has a lot to do with how well you control the density of the food that fills that one-litre space. It's hard to visualise this concept as food is always displayed in terms of grams on packaging rather than volume. Instead, let's use drinks to illustrate this point. At one end of a spectrum, you have water which has zero calories. At the other end of the scale a milkshake can have over a thousand calories of energy per litre. Both drinks will occupy the same litre of space available in the stomach. The milkshake will provide nearly half of the energy required for a sedentary adult for a day. The water will provide no energy whatsoever. Apply this logic to the food that you eat. All food occupies a certain amount of space in the stomach. For this given amount of space some foods will provide a lot more energy than others. During the first stages of digestion, you chew and massage food down into a pulp to best fill the limited space in the stomach. This is very important when food isn't easily digestible. Processed food has become more easily digestible to allow you to eat more and process it quicker. Requiring you to refill more frequently. Your body still relies on hunger cues that come largely from feelings of fullness. Modern food can leave you feeling hungry again sooner than the need to replenish the energy you have burned since your last meal.

You will use the proportion of macronutrients to set the structure of your diet. Opting for foods that are quality sources of protein, carbohydrate, and fat. There are two reasons why a macronutrient plan is ideal. Firstly, you want to ensure you are getting the right nutrients in the right ratios. Secondly, by setting moderate goals for protein, carbohydrates and fats means that you eliminate the risk of cutting out vital nutrients from any one group. If one of these nutrients falls too low the body will make compensations elsewhere. Balancing your nutrition is not just about making sure you get enough of one nutrient; it is making sure you don't do that at the expense of other nutrients.

First, let's look at the importance of protein and set some protein goals.

PROTEIN

Muscle along with many other tissues in the body is made predominantly of protein. Protein is made up of amino acids, when proteins are built from amino acids this is known as protein synthesis. The two amino acids that make up 90% of muscle tissue are actin and myosin.

When amino acids are made from breaking down proteins this is known as protein breakdown. The net difference between protein synthesis and breakdown is known as protein balance. Changes in lean mass will typically reflect overall protein balance. Some amino acids are non-essential and can be synthesised in the body from other amino acids. There are nine essential amino acids must be regularly consumed. Including the most abundant amino acids in muscle tissues, the branched-chain amino acids: leucine, valine, and isoleucine. Even though there are essential amino acids that must be consumed in the diet, only a fraction of the overall daily protein intake contributes to the total turnover of amino acids. There is a large pool of amino acids in the body as well as the constant resynthesizing of amino acids from other amino acids. Protein turnover is the sum of all protein degradation and protein synthesis.

A typical man will consume enough protein to cover protein turnover, any excess being turned into either new amino acids or other chemicals in the body such as serotonin. Excess amino acids that cannot be used are broken down into ammonia and urea and are filtered out of the bloodstream via the kidneys. It is important to maintain hydration if you are increasing your protein intake to reduce the strain on your kidneys.

I am going to give you a simple calculation to calculate your optimal protein intake later in this section. It is worth noting that although your protein intake is suboptimal for someone who exercises regularly, your protein intake is sufficient to cover protein synthesis for the time-being. You can gradually increase your protein intake steadily to a more optimal level. Not try to make a sea-change overnight.

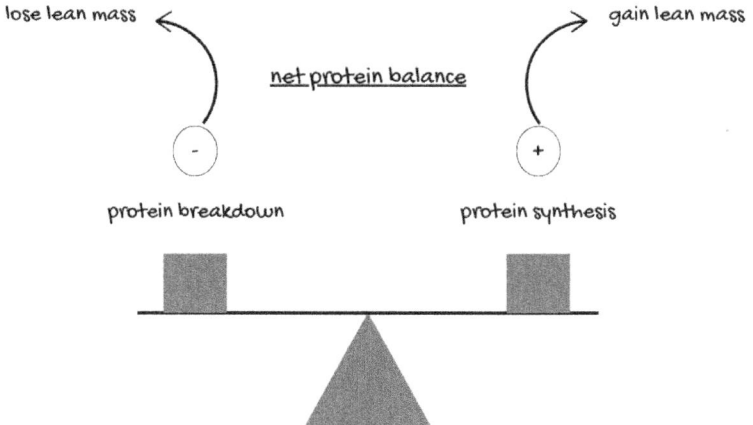

A calorie-restricted diet restricts all nutrients, protein intake included. You can guard against this by monitoring your protein intake when you are dieting. The most abundant source of protein being meat, fish, and dairy, if meat, fish and dairy intake is reduced, so too is protein intake. Resistance training places larger demands of protein on the body, to maintain a positive protein balance protein intake needs to be increased. The rate of protein breakdown remains constant however resistance training increases protein synthesis. Resistance training creates more demand for new protein. The combination of resistance training and protein intake are what are required to achieve a positive protein balance and build new muscle mass.

Protein intake is usually prescribed as a multiplier of your body weight. For new clients, I used to recommend they take their body weight in kilograms and double it. That's how much protein they should be eating per day. But I had a problem when I started training men who were 40% body fat or higher. My recommendations could be 250+ grams of protein per day. From someone eating barely 50 grams of protein per day that is an unimaginable jump! This recommendation was based on what was being recommended to athletes. Most athletes are leaner than your typical man, let alone your man trying to drop significant body fat. It was thought that there was a direct correlation between body weight and the amount of protein you should be eating. Protein intake would be exaggerated as body weight and body fat percentage increases, so we needed a better guide. Most athletes have low body fat percentages. The recommendation should have been for lean mass not total body weight. Lean mass is directly correlated to muscle mass as mineral mass is constant. Therefore, the more lean mass someone has the more muscle mass they typically have. Protein intake should correlate with lean mass, rather than body weight. This should make sense as the more lean mass you have the more protein you need to consume to maintain it. Take your lean mass, not your body weight, and double it. This should be your daily protein intake.

The goal is to maintain protein synthesis whether you are trying to lose fat mass or gain muscle mass or both. A positive protein balance is ideal. When building muscle, the benefits of a positive protein balance are obvious. You will be building new muscle tissue. However, when trying to lose fat mass you are trying to negate protein breakdown and losing muscle tissue. This will result in a higher p-ratio, larger net protein loss relative to fat mass loss, and is bad news. You can achieve this by keeping quality protein intake moderate and frequent throughout the day. Extreme diets of fasting and gorging are clearly suboptimal. You will be spending long periods of time fasted and in a negative net protein balance. Followed by short periods of excessive protein to synthesise in one go. A large proportion will end up being either used for other things or broken down and excreted. Avoid this by keeping your protein intake steady. A meal every 3-6 hours that you are awake is ideal.

Protein foods, such as meat and dairy, don't contain 100% protein. A 250g steak is not 250g of protein. It is helpful to know the amounts of protein in some common foods (see the table below). Just like we did with calories, we will split the daily target further into targets per meal. Depending on how many meals per day you want to have will dictate how large a serving of protein you will have per meal. You may find it easier to break your day into more meals to make the portion of protein more manageable. Our 95-kilogram man who has 66 kilograms of lean mass will have a protein target of 132 grams of protein per day. Split this into four meals means 33 grams of protein per meal. Using the table below you can see that 110 grams of chicken breast for one of those meals would be perfect. The other meals could be made up of 300 grams of egg whites, 120 grams of tinned tuna, 50 grams of whey powder or 110 grams of beef mince. If some meals are over, then other meals can be pulled back. You don't have to divide your protein intake perfectly evenly per meal. Consistency helps in the early days before changing things. Commit to a handful of protein sources that are regulars at each meal.

Use packaging to give you a *per cent* view of protein. You can look at the per 100g column on the nutritional information table. Anything that doesn't come pre-packaged, then you can do a quick google for typical amounts. If you shop at a butcher's shop. Fresh foods that don't come with labels aren't usually the foods that

trip people up!

	Per 100g / Percent.			
	Carb.	Protein	Fat	Kcal
5% Beef Mince	0.0	31.0	4.7	166.0
Beef Fillet Steak	0.0	27.2	6.7	171.1
Chicken Breast	0.0	30.1	1.1	131.0
Cod Fillet	0.0	21.5	1.3	98.0
Egg Whites	0.8	10.9	0.0	48.0
Icelandic Natural Yoghurt	4.0	11.0	0.2	65.0
Tinned Tuna	0.0	27.0	0.0	113.0
Tofu	1.8	11.9	6.8	118.0
Tuna Steak	0.0	33.0	1.6	148.0
Whey Powder	8.2	70.0	9.0	401.0

This isn't an exhaustive list but rather to give you an idea of some popular protein foods. For a more expansive list go to intelligentshedder.com/tools.

To give you an example, 100g of chicken breast contains 30% or 30g of protein. Not to mention it has 1.1% fat making it a popular choice. It will also contain 68.9g of non-energetic mass, meaning it has a low energy density but high protein content. Perfect!

For each meal, pick one protein food as the main part of your meal. You now have the first part of your macro-based nutrition plan. In the following chapters we will look at the other nutrients and their sources to build a healthy meal plan.

Action Steps

1. Calculate your protein intake by multiplying your lean mass by 2.

2. Divide your daily protein intake across your meal frequency.

3. Select your protein sources that provide this much protein per meal.

As fat goes hand in hand with protein, some of your protein sources will also be a source of fat. Let's look at fat next.

FAT

A common misconception is that dietary fat and body fat are the same thing, sparking the low-fat movement. You now know that body fat is the storage of excess energy from protein, fat, carbohydrates, and alcohol. If you have an excess of any of the above macronutrients, converting them into fatty acids and storing inside fat cells is the safest and most efficient way to store them. Glucose can be the intermediary in this process, causing the demonisation of carbohydrates as well as fat!

Approximately 98% of the total energy stores in the body are stored as fats. That's more than fifty times the energy that is stored as carbohydrates. The biggest fat store in the body is the layer of subcutaneous fat that is just under the skin. When fat is broken down to be used for energy it is split into two parts: glycerol and fatty acids. The glycerol is then transported to the liver and converted into glucose to be used. The fatty acids can be transported directly to muscle tissue. Fatty acids in the muscle tissue, including those transported from the subcutaneous fat can be oxidised to produce energy.

The second misconception is that there are different heart rate zones that have some bearing on overall fat loss. But this is missing the woods for the trees because we are attempting to change chronic body fat levels. You will be making withdrawals from your fat stores over several weeks regardless of the energetic demands you place within a workout. Even when glucose is used as a fuel source it is replenished by glycerol from stored body fat. This means that whatever you burn in a workout, is fuelled by your fat stores when dietary energy is deficient. As the energy provided by the diet is inadequate, the body becomes more reliant on energy from fat stores. Maintaining an energy deficit through a moderate diet and increased activity will keep the demand on body fat stores. For energy used for everything from exercise to daily tasks. The only way you're going to make a significant dent in your body fat is by a sustained energy deficit that is consistently withdrawing from your fat stores.

Fat isn't only important for energy; fat has other structural uses for important organs such as the brain and constructing hormones. Remember, an optimal hormonal environment is essential for building muscle. If the body doesn't have the essential fats to build hormones, then muscle building will be limited. Some vitamins also aren't soluble in water and therefore need fat present to be absorbed by the body. These are known as the fat-soluble vitamins (A, D, E and K). Some essential fatty acids, like essential amino acids, cannot be synthesised in the body and therefore must come from the diet. These essential fatty acids are important in the processes mentioned above. A suboptimal fat intake will result in poorer health. Essential fatty acids can be supplemented as Omega-3 essential fatty acids: eicosapentaenoic acid (EPA) and docosahexaenoic acid (DHA).

Ask any chef and they will tell you that fat is important for flavour and texture of foods. Fats should be included in a diet to maintain enjoyment. Meat and fish can become quite dry and boring without it.

	Per 100g / Percent.			
	Carb.	Protein	Fat	Kcal
Pork Shoulder Steak	0.6	27.8	16.9	276.0
Sardines	1.2	27.7	18.4	282.0
Sea Bass	0.0	25.9	9.8	194.4
Bacon Rashers	1.0	25.8	13.8	233.0
Salmon Fillet	0.0	25.5	9.8	191.0
Cheddar Cheese	0.1	25.4	34.9	416.0
12% Beef Mince	0.0	25.0	11.8	206.0
Beef Rump Steak	0.6	24.3	15.5	239.0
Sirloin Beef Steak	0.0	16.6	22.8	272.0
Mackerel Fillet	0.0	15.7	24.5	285.0
Greek Yoghurt	5.3	5.0	9.7	129.0

A moderate target of fat intake is 20% of your total calorie intake. You need to know how much energy fat contains. One gram of fat contains 9 kilocalories of energy. You can convert your calories from fat to grams of fat quite simply by dividing by nine. For example, a 2,000-kilocalorie diet with 20% of its energy coming from dietary fat means 400 kcal from fat. 400 kcal of fat is equal to 44 grams of fat.

	Per 100g / Percent.			
	Carb.	Protein	Fat	Kcal
90% Cocoa Chocolate	14.0	10.0	55.0	592
Almonds	13.3	29.0	49.2	626
Avocado	1.9	1.9	19.5	198
Butter	0.6	0.6	81.0	734
Coconut Oil	0.0	0.0	100.0	899
Flaxseed Oil	0.0	0.0	92.8	835
Goats Cheese	1.4	14.0	27.7	312
Sunflower Seeds	16.4	23.4	47.5	599
Virgin Olive Oil	0.0	0.0	91.5	823
Walnuts	3.1	17.3	68.5	707

Most of your dietary fat will be combined with fatty protein sources such as beef. Beef mince, and other minced meat, are simple protein sources as they come in clear levels of fat content. 5% mince is considered lean mince. 10-15% fat content is considered moderate, and 20% fat content could be considered high fat.

The remainder of your fat intake should come from a range of minimally processed fats, such as nuts, seeds, and oils. Synthesised trans fats, such as margarine and those used in deep fat fryers should be avoided as much as possible. Fat contains twice the energy per gram than protein and carbohydrate. It is important to keep an eye on fat sources to ensure that calories aren't inadvertently going out of control. As a significant amount of your fats will come from fattier protein sources, add high fat foods sparingly. A little will go a long way. For example, coconut oil is 100% fat, therefore 10g of coconut oil will add 10g of fat to your fat intake.

By removing the visible fat from fattier cuts of meat you will reduce the fat content approximately by half. This is a helpful strategy for controlling your fat intake if needed. If you swap one of your lean protein sources for one of these fattier sources, you will probably find it easier to be able to achieve your daily fat goal.

Action Steps

1. Calculate your fat intake by multiplying your total daily calories by 0.2.

2. Divide your calorie allocation for fat by 9 to calculate your grams of fat per day.

3. Divide your daily fat intake across your meal frequency.

4. Select your fatty protein sources and fat sources that provide this much fat per meal.

Next, we will look at the one macronutrient that we don't set a target for, but you need to know about.

ALCOHOL

I have included alcohol after the fat chapter because although it is not a macronutrient that we will set as a goal it still has to be accounted for. Alcohol is converted into fat in the liver; the outcome of alcohol intake is fat synthesis. This is how alcohol which is toxic is stabilised and the excess energy from alcohol is stored. Excess alcohol consumption leads to fatty liver disease.

The recommendation for health is no more than fourteen units of alcohol per week, spread across at least three sittings. No more than about five units or two pints of beer or a large glass of wine. My first recommendation depends on what your current alcohol intake is. Firstly, if your alcohol intake is above the recommended amount my advice is to reduce it to within recommended levels. This will have obvious health benefits and reduce your excessive calorie intake significantly. Then to reduce your calorie intake further you can reduce your alcohol intake to the level that you feel appropriate. If you want to cut out alcohol completely then that's up to you. If you can manage it within your calories, then this can provide a mental boost. One glass of wine per week with a meal should be plenty, but if it's managed within your calories, it's entirely up to you. There is no specific goal for alcohol. You will have to account for the calories from your fat and carbohydrate intake. The easy way is to account for your overall calorie intake and your protein intake. Carbohydrates, fat and alcohol will make up whatever calories are left. This is not a strategy you want to use too often. Only on the odd days you must. This means that by drinking alcohol you get to eat less. A less ideal situation.

Action Steps

1. Estimate your alcohol intake per week and per drinking session.

2. Plan to reduce your intake to less than 14 units per week and less than five units per session.

3. Can you reduce it to one drink per week or less?

Next, we're going to discuss the final macronutrient, carbohydrates.

CARBOHYDRATES

Most short-term energy comes from glucose, a short form carbohydrate. Glucose can be created from the breakdown of longer carbohydrates or can be produced from amino acids and fatty acids (gluconeogenesis). Because glucose can be produced from non-carbohydrate sources it is often considered non-essential. Carbohydrates are still important in many processes in the body, not to mention the most common fuel in muscle tissue. To reduce carbohydrate intake to suboptimal levels would negatively affect training and your results.

Carbohydrates come in chains of different lengths. Both glucose and fructose are hexoses, six carbon carbohydrates. Simple carbohydrates, called sugars, give you energy more immediately. Simple carbohydrates can be beneficial around training when fuel requirements are more urgent. More complex carbohydrates are longer chains of sugars that take longer to break down and to release their energy. The complexity of carbohydrates can be scored according to the extent to which they increase blood glucose levels. This is known as the glycaemic index (GI). Low GI foods such as fruits and vegetables will raise blood glucose by a small degree over a longer period. High GI foods such as fruit juices and processed sugars will provide a spike of glucose in the bloodstream. Simple sugars are great for fuelling exercise but are an inefficient way of fuelling the body outside of exercise sessions. Try to keep all carbohydrates to low GI to provide a steady fuel supply throughout the day to avoid peaks and crashes.

You've already calculated your calories, protein and fat targets. Calculating your carbohydrate target is easy!

Carbohydrates will make up the remaining calories when protein and fat have been accounted for.

To calculate your carbohydrate target, first remove the 20% of your calories given to fat. You are now working with the remaining 80% of your total calorie target, which are your calories for protein and carbohydrates. Subtract your protein target as calories. Multiply your protein target in grams by 4. This gives you your protein target in calories. Remember, every gram of protein is four calories of energy. Subtract your protein calories from your calorie total. The calories that are left are for your carbohydrates. Similarly to protein, carbohydrates also have 4 calories per gram. Divide the remaining calories by four to get your carbohydrates target in grams.

To give you an example; our 90-kilogram man who has a calorie target of 2,000 calories, will have 1,600 calories for protein and carbohydrates. I have removed the 400 calories (44 grams) of fat. Next you take his protein target which is 132 grams (528 calories) of protein. Leaving 1,072 calories for carbohydrates. If you divide 1,072 by four, he will have a target of 268 grams of carbohydrates per day. 89 grams of carbohydrates per meal for three meals a day, or 67 grams of carbohydrates per meal for four meals per day or 45 grams per meal for six meals per day. Just like the other macronutrients, the ideal frequency and size of meals per day is a personal preference. Go with what is enjoyable and suits your lifestyle the best.

Now, let's look at where to get carbohydrates from. Quality carbohydrate sources will provide a variety of micronutrients as well. Glucose can be synthesised from other nutrients in the body. A lot of micronutrients that you get with the carbohydrates cannot. These foods are important for more reasons beyond providing a source of fuel. It is why I have presented fruits and vegetables before grains. The more of your carbohydrates you can gain from fruits and vegetables the more micronutrients you will also get.

The low-carb movement made a lot of people fear fruit. However, fruit is very low in calorie density. Looking at the table above, not a single fruit is more than 23% carbohydrate. Some berries and citrus fruits are as low as 3-4% carbohydrate, they also pack so many more micronutrients.

	Per 100g / Percent.			
	Carb.	Protein	Fat	Kcal
Banana	23.2	1.2	0.0	103
Blueberries	9.1	0.9	0.0	45
Green Apple	11.8	0.0	0.0	53
Kiwi	11.0	1.1	0.0	55
Lemon	3.0	1.0	0.0	19
Limes	3.2	1.0	0.0	20
Pear	10.0	0.0	0.0	40
Pineapple	10.1	0.4	0.2	40
Raspberries	4.6	1.4	0.0	32
Red Apple	11.8	0.0	0.0	47
Red/Black Grapes	17.0	0.6	0.0	75
Satsumas	9.6	0.7	0.0	45
White Grapes	15.4	0.0	0.0	66

Apples have approximately 50 kilocalories per 100g; a calorie density of 0.5. A cookie can have ten times the calories and five times the amount of sugar as an apple. But the low carb movement groups all these foods together and would have you believe that they are the same. Not only are the macronutrient profiles very different, but you also get many vitamins and minerals from fruits. Unprocessed carbohydrates are lower in GI and contain less protein and fat and are less calorie dense.

	Per 100g / Percent.			
	Carb.	Protein	Fat	Kcal
Aubergine	3.1	0.5	0.2	22
Broccoli	3.1	4.3	0.6	40
Carrots	5.6	0.6	0.2	33
Celery	1.1	1.1	0.2	13
Courgette	1.8	1.8	0.0	20
Cucumber	1.4	0.7	0.0	11
Green Beans	4.0	2.1	0.0	37
Kale	1.3	3.4	1.6	39
Lettuce	1.3	1.2	0.0	14
Onions	7.6	1.0	0.0	38
Peas	9.4	5.1	0.4	69
Peppers	2.6	0.8	0.3	15
Red Cabbage	3.5	1.6	0.2	26
Tomatoes	3.1	0.7	0.0	20

The carbohydrates in vegetables are practically negligible. Vegetables not only provide low GI carbohydrates, but they will massively decrease the calorie density of a meal. The more vegetables you add, the less the density of the calories of the overall meal. This is one thing that is seldom capitalised on those dieting. They will give themselves a calorie target and try to fit the foods they are used to into this reduced target. By adding vegetables to your meals, you will increase the volume of food you are eating. Taking up more space in your stomach leaving you feeling fuller for longer for the same number of calories.

Fruits and vegetables will contain a lot of fibre which is important for gut health. Fibre is important for clearing the bowels, maintaining an efficient digestive system, and reducing cancer risk.

The remainder of your carbohydrates can come from grains such as breads, pasta, and rice. We are not trying to eradicate carbohydrates entirely from the diet. You need carbohydrates to maintain fibre intake and to provide energy, so you don't feel sluggish or drowsy or train poorly.

	Per 100g / Percent.			
	Carb.	Protein	Fat	Kcal
Basmati Rice*	80.2	8.6	0.9	370
Brown Rice*	55.4	8.2	2.7	289
Cornflakes	84.0	7.0	0.9	378
Granola	66.2	7.8	12.2	419
Muesli	57.9	10.1	11.0	389
Porridge Oats*	60.5	10.3	7.0	363
Rice Noodles*	82.0	6.4	0.0	356
Sourdough Bread	45.1	9.8	2.8	250
Sweet Potato	20.0	1.6	0.0	91
Weetabix	69.0	12.0	2.0	362
White Potato	17.5	2.0	0.0	81
White Rice*	68.5	7.1	1.1	318
Whole Wheat Pasta*	67.0	11.6	2.0	349
Wholemeal Bread	39.3	9.6	3.2	239
Wholemeal Wraps	45.0	8.7	6.4	288

The foods in the above list have an asterisk (*) if they are dry weights. When they are rehydrated, they will likely double in volume. For example, 50 grams of white rice will give you approximately 35 grams of carbohydrate.

When rice is rehydrated, it doubles in volume, but the calorie and macronutrients stay the same. Only the water content has been increased. One hundred grams of cooked rice has the same nutrient content as fifty grams of uncooked rice. This is worth bearing in mind when you think about the calorie density of carbohydrates, make sure you consider them in the form that you eat them!

The best way to measure grains is to consistently use a measuring cup. Weigh a cup of grains the first time and then use the same cup each time. If a measuring cup measures 50 grams of oats, each time you use the same measuring cup you are getting 50 grams of oats. You don't have to weigh the oats every time. Measuring cups are cheap. I store my rice, pasta and oats in jars and leave the measuring cup in the jar with them. Once I've measured, I keep using the same cup.

Action Steps

1. Calculate your target calories for carbohydrate and protein by multiplying your total calorie target by 0.8.

2. Minus your protein target in grams multiplied by four to get your carbohydrate target in calories.

3. Divide your carbohydrate target in calories by four to get your carbohydrate target in grams.

4. Divide your daily carbohydrate intake across your meal frequency.

5. Select your carbohydrate sources prioritising fruits and vegetables that provide this much carbohydrate per meal.

Next, let's put everything together to create your personalised nutrition plan.

YOUR NUTRITION PLAN

There are quite a few steps in this chapter that I don't want to get lost in all the information, I thought I'd circle round and list the important steps in one place. Then I've provided some example nutrition plans.

Step 1. Getting Started

- Keep a food log of everything you eat.

- Count the total 'minimally processed foods' and 'ultra-processed foods'.

- Create a repertoire of healthy go-to meals using minimally processed foods.

Step 2. Calculating your calories

- Calculate your resting energy expenditure (REE)

- Calculate your activity level (AL)

- Calculate your total daily energy expenditure (TDEE = REE x AL)

- Calculate your energy deficit.

- Calculate your daily energy intake.

Step 3. Protein

- Calculate your protein intake by multiplying your lean mass by 2.

- Divide your daily protein intake across your meal frequency.

- Select your protein sources that provide this much protein per meal.

Step 4. Fat

- Calculate your fat intake by multiplying your total daily calories by 0.2.

- Divide your calorie allocation for fat by 9 to calculate your grams of fat per day.

- Divide your daily fat intake across your meal frequency.

- Select your fatty protein sources and fat sources that provide this much fat per meal.

Step 5. Alcohol

- Estimate your alcohol intake per week and per drinking session.
- Plan to reduce your intake to less than 14 units per week and less than five units per session.
- Can you reduce it to one drink per week or less?

Step 6. Carbohydrates

- Calculate your target calories for carbohydrate and protein by multiplying your total calorie target by 0.8.
- Minus your protein target in grams multiplied by four to get your carbohydrate target in calories.
- Divide your carbohydrate target in calories by four to get your carbohydrate in grams.
- Divide your daily carbohydrate intake across your meal frequency.
- Select your carbohydrate sources prioritising fruits and vegetables that provide this much carbohydrate per meal.

My nutrition plan:

I will burn _____ kcal of energy per day.

I will eat _____ kcal of energy per day, as…

_____ grams of protein per day, across _____ meals.

_____ grams of fat per day, across _____ meals.

_____ grams of carbohydrate per day, across _____ meals.

Meal One

One poached egg

Two slices of bacon medallions

One slice of wholemeal toast

10g of butter

Meal Two

35g of whey protein

Medium banana

Meal Three

One chicken breast

65g of basmati rice

Handful of salad leaves

Chopped salad vegetables (carrot, celery, peppers, cucumber, baby radishes etc.)

30g of feta cheese

Meal Four

125g of 5% beef mince (fried in 5 ml of olive oil)

Tinned chopped tomatoes.

White onion, carrot, celery

Italian herbs (oregano, basil, rosemary, bay)

75g of wholemeal pasta

A QUICK ASK

Before we dive into the training section, I have a small favour to ask. If you've made it this far, chances are you've already found value in this book. Whether it's the clarity around measurements or the simplicity of the nutrition framework. Maybe you've even started applying some of the strategies and are seeing changes already.

Here's the deal: books like this thrive on feedback. Your experience matters - not just to me, but to the countless people who are searching for a resource that works. By leaving a review on Amazon, you're not only helping this book reach more people, but you're also helping others take control of their fitness journey.

It doesn't take long. Just head over to Amazon, find this book, and click "Write a Review." Be honest - share what stood out, what you've learned, or how it's impacted you. It could be one line or a few paragraphs - whatever you feel like sharing.

This book is my way of paying it forward. I've poured years of experience into these pages to help you get real, measurable results. If it's made a difference for you, leaving a review is the best way to say thank you - and it'll inspire me to keep creating resources like this.

So, before you dive into creating your personalised training plan, take a moment to help someone else start their journey too.

SECTION 3 - TRAINING

The training that you do sends the stimulus for your body to change physically; nothing will occur without a stimulus. The body simply has no reason to change unless it is stimulated to. This explains why some people fail to get results at all and why others find their results plateau. The stimulus they are creating has dropped below a threshold required where change is stimulated.

Exercise is a stress. You are attempting to stress your system into adapting. It is an evolutionary process that it's not the strongest that survive but those most able to adapt to their environment. By exercising you are creating an artificial stressful environment for your body to adapt to. This was first discovered nearly a hundred years ago by Austrian Canadian endocrinologist Hans Selye. Organisms go through three distinct phases when dealing with stress. Initially there is the Alarm phase, this is the initial 'in-the-moment' response. We call this an acute response, you will often see it referred to as fight, flight, or freeze. There is a clear physiological response: sweating, increased breathing, blood pressure and heart rate, and heightened alertness. If the stress goes away the body returns to its normal state, rest, and digest, relatively quickly. All the above symptoms happen when we work out. This stress response is uncomfortable, workouts are hard; particularly the first one. No wonder some never return after the first session, everything inside them is telling them to get away, their survival depends on it.

If the stress continues, the organism passes into the second phase, the resistance phase. The stress isn't going anywhere in the short term, so the organism has to adapt to the stress. The organism knows that it is highly likely to continue to experience the stress. If you train frequently enough, then your body will start to adapt to the stress of exercise to make following exercise sessions easier. This is where exercisers are trying to maintain their training. Constantly moving the goalposts so that you can continue adapting. If the organism fails to adapt in the resistance phase or it simply doesn't have the resources to cope the stress becomes overwhelming and the organism passes into the third and final phase, the exhaustion phase. This happens when all the resources have been spent and the organism can no longer resist the stress. This is where either serious injury or illness puts the brakes on, or the organism dies. Managing stress is like surfing a wave. You need enough stress to put you into the resistance phase so that adaptation occurs, but not so much that you become ill or injured. Being in the resistance phase doesn't mean the alarm phase has ended, you will still experience an acute response to every training session. The response to multiple sessions being adaptation. Maintaining the training stress is like being in control of the flame of a hot air balloon, you need to blast short bursts of gas, but also to space out the burst so you don't run out of gas prematurely.

Another analogy I always like to use is responding to exercise like getting a suntan. You must go into the sun to get a tan first and foremost; you can't ever get a tan if you stay in the shade. However, sun exposure on your skin is a stress, everyone has different capacities for dealing with the stress of the sun. Going in the sun for too long, or when it's too intense will cause exhaustion, ranging from sun burn to heat stroke. Never going in the sun will result in pasty white skin. You won't maintain a suntan just from one exposure to the sun, it's all about managing the dose, the goldilocks effect of not too little and not too much. Exercise is the same. People overestimate the effect of a single session but dramatically underestimate the effect of multiple well-timed sessions at the correct intensity. Little to no adaptation will occur from a single session. If anything, that's just your body showing where it currently is physiologically. It's not known where the next stress will be from this one single data point. The body being a fickle thing will hedge its bets on what is most economical. You will not adapt from one single bout of exercise. After the first few weeks of training most of the changes in strength occur from neurological changes. The body gets more organised. It can recruit muscle fibres with more ease and coordination. You need these changes so that you can train with increased strength to start to ask more of your muscles. Lifting more so that adaptation is a possibility. Finally, after a few weeks the changes are mostly physical, new structures are being built to better handle stress in the future. Bigger muscles can create and overcome greater forces therefore muscles need to develop to handle more stress.

One final note on the work of Hans Selye. If exercise were the only stress, you were experiencing it would be really easy to monitor the dose. However, you will have other stresses in your life that will also test your capabilities and drain your resources for dealing with stress. According the Benenden Health the ten most stressful life events are as follows[12]:

1. The death of a family member or friend.

2. Financial challenges.

3. Issues at work.

4. Change in a relationship.

5. Divorce.

6. Exams & studying.

7. Buying a house.

8. Reading/watching the news.

9. Having a child.

10. Starting a new job.

This survey was conducted with 2,000 normal Brits, so chances are you too will experience one or more of the above life events. It's important to have a plan that is flexible to appreciate the other stress in your life, and one you can stick to and enjoy even in tough times.

---

[12] https://www.benenden.co.uk/newsroom/top-ten-most-stressful-life-events/

In the following chapters we will discuss the stimuli for burning fat and building muscle. To burn fat, you need to stimulate your body to use up its fat reserves. Don't believe the nonsense you read about the body holding onto 'stubborn fat' the purpose of fat is stored energy. Create a demand for that energy and it will be happily given up.

Secondly, regardless of whether you want to add pounds of muscle or not you will always want to stimulate your body to regenerate muscle tissue. The training stimulus is the same. We will look at this in more detail. You don't become a ripped freak by accident just by lifting weights. Just like you don't become a world class racing driver by accident just by driving to work. Never curtail your own training just because you don't want to become 'too developed'.

Next, let's look at the stimulus needed to burn fat, stubborn included.

FAT LOSS

As we covered in the nutrition section the fat stores around your body are the storage vessels for excess energy that has been taken on board. Like an accountant's ledger, all the energy that comes in and leaves the body must be accounted for. Once you have anchored your energy intake to between your resting energy expenditure (REE) and total daily energy expenditure (TDEE), you can increase your expenditure through exercise to moderate the speed of fat loss.

As we've already established, fat loss is stimulated by creating a deficit between energy intake and energy expenditure. In the previous section we established that this can be done without increasing expenditure by reducing intake. This is the classic *diet only*; using diet alone to burn fat. You're restricting your energy intake to stimulate your body to make up the shortfall from its fat reserves. Although sound in principle this is often poorly executed. Remember the activity level table? You will burn your resting energy expenditure with zero activity. A sedentary person will burn 20% above their REE. An average expenditure should be around 55% above REE and so on. Without exercise your expenditure is capped at approximately 20% above your REE, so your margins in which to create a deficit are very small. This also gives you very little leeway should you go 'off-plan'. The result is either no fat loss because the deficit is too easy to fill in, or you must cut food intake lower until the point the whole thing becomes miserable, and you give up.

The intelligent way to set your energy intake is to anchor your calories to a fixed number, higher than your REE, and then add a calorie deficit on top. The benefit of this is that you can eat everything you want and still lose weight. This is done by maintaining your current eating habits but increasing your energy expenditure. Whether you reduce your intake by 500 kcal or increase your energy expenditure by 500 kcal the result is still a 500 kcal deficit. You probably spend most of the year 'weight stable'. A small portion of the year, such as holidays, your weight will increase and some of the year your weight will drop. You're not consistently gaining weight week in week out. A typical week will mean your weight stays the same. So if you were to keep your eating habits the same, but increase your expenditure you are guaranteed fat loss.

Now we will focus on how you increase your calorie expenditure to increase your calorie deficit. This will be done by anchoring your calorie intake and increasing your expenditure. Once you have built exercise into your routine and you enjoy it, you will use those workouts to increase your expenditure upwards. Not as most coaches promote, drop calories when you hit a plateau.

You can swap an extreme diet or exercise routine for a moderate combination of diet and exercise and get the same results in fat loss. A lot of people forget this when they see their fat loss slow down. They have only focused on what they eat and forgotten the impact of how much they move has on fat loss. They may still be eating as well as they were when they started, but their activity may have slowed down and vice versa. Just like a seesaw, you can tip the see-saw by adding weight to one end or lightening the other end. Only focusing on how much weight is on one end of the see-saw irrespective of what's on the other end won't necessarily move it. If your fat loss has stalled it's because you've slipped back into a balance of energy. The exact amount of energy that your diet is deficient in, the calorie deficit, is how much energy will be taken out of your energy stores. To recap from the previous section, but from the perspective of exercise. Body fat is the easiest way for our body to lock away energy for the medium to long term. Every kilogram of body fat we are carrying is holding 7,700 kcal of energy. Enough for just over ten hours of moderate exercise. We dip into these stores whenever we exercise and don't fully replenish them again with the food we eat. When you exercise you aren't burning 100% fat, the energy you are using is coming from a mixture of sources. This is true at rest and exercising as hard as you can. 50-60% of the energy you burn during exercise comes from fat. This will drop significantly as exercise intensity increases. I'll explain why later. Too many people get caught up trying to find the sweet spot of fat burning during their sessions. This is missing the woods for the trees because if you are maintaining an energy deficit all calories will lead to fat loss. All energy is replenished from your long-term energy stores, body fat. Even if you are burning predominantly glycogen (carbohydrates) at a high exercise intensity this glycogen will be replenished from fat stores via gluconeogenesis. I always like to compare it to a hybrid engine. You use one fuel source most of the time, like the electric battery, until either it reaches its work capacity, or it needs to be replenished. Then an alternative energy source kicks into action, like the petrol engine. Although our bodies are of course much more complex and rather than two energy systems there are multiple. You don't switch between different systems. They are all running simultaneously. At different times each system will provide more or less energy depending on the situation. This is where the idea of different 'zones' is misleading. You are always burning fat as a fuel, just like you are always burning carbohydrates and amino acids as fuel. But different intensities place different demands on the different energy systems. We will go into energy systems in more detail in the next chapter, but for now understand this; even if you burn predominantly carbohydrates in an intense training session, those carbohydrates, as well as the energy they provide, will need to be replenished. If our diet following this exercise session doesn't fully replenish these stores body fat will be broken down to make up the difference. A consistent energy deficit over time will lead to a consistent drawing down on fat reserves.

There are two ways to achieve an energy deficit. You can either keep your activity levels the same. Remember if you are sedentary this is 20% above your resting expenditure and cut your food intake by the required number of calories. Or you can keep your food intake the same, and you can increase your calorie expenditure by the required number of calories through new activity. Whilst mechanically this model is perfect and you can estimate the number of calories required to lose a certain amount of body fat (approximately 7,700kcal). Being a human means you likely will have to deal with increased hunger, cravings, and reduced energy. Exercise has been shown to largely offset the negative effects of diet on hunger, cravings, and energy. Research shows that a combination of moderate exercise and diet to be most effective in reducing body fat whilst reducing the negative side-effects of dieting.

In the 20th century a compendium was compiled to compare every activity possible against resting energy expenditure. This is known as the Metabolic Equivalent of Tasks (METs). This should sound familiar, to calculate your calorie expenditure you multiplied your resting energy expenditure by an average for the whole 24-hour day. You can take this a step further by calculating the approximate expenditure of different activities, per hour, by grouping them together. When you are asleep you are burning 90% of your REE, Activities where you are sitting you are burning 110% of your REE. When you are standing you are burning 150-200% of your REE and walking will burn 200-300% of your REE. When I cycle to the gym at an average of 15 miles per hour (10 METS) for twenty minutes I am expending the same energy as when I lift weights (3.5 METS) during a 60-minute session. That means cycling can burn three times the energy of lifting weights.

Let's investigate why:

$$\left(\frac{REE}{24}\right) \times \left(\frac{MET \times Duration\ (mins)}{60}\right)$$

$$= Energy\ expended$$

$$\left(\frac{1,799}{24}\right) \times \left(\frac{10 \times 20}{60}\right) = 273 KCal\ burned\ cycling$$

$$\left(\frac{1,799}{24}\right) \times \left(\frac{3.5 \times 60}{60}\right)$$

$$= 248 KCal\ burned\ lifting\ weights$$

You need to turn our daily REE into an hourly REE so the first thing you do is to divide your REE by 24. Then you multiply the MET score by the minutes you do it for, divided by the 60 minutes in an hour. Then multiply the two together to get an estimation of the energy expended during that session. As you can see above, 20 minutes cycling at 15 miles per hour expends as much energy as resistance training for 60 minutes. Weights are often misquoted as burning more calories but that's because rests aren't usually factored into the calculations. The calories burned during a weights session is considerably lower than what is commonly reported.

The above results are the acute results, the body will become more efficient at not only oxidising fat but also endurance exercise itself. This allows you to burn fuel more efficiently and faster, for longer. Allowing you to push your limits further. Remember the body is adapting to the stress you place on it to better equip you, and allow you to do more, in future training sessions.

Let's look at energy systems in more detail to understand how the body creates energy for exercise.

ENERGY SYSTEMS

All muscular contraction and thus movement is powered by a molecule called adenosine triphosphate (ATP). ATP is basically the currency of human movement. ATP is an adenosine molecule with a tail of three phosphates. An enzyme called ATPase breaks off the end phosphate, releasing an explosion of energy that is used to power movement such as a muscular contraction.

There are three energy systems that create ATP. First, the Alactic (ATP-PC) system uses the ATP that is already stored in muscle cells for the first two seconds of maximum intensity action. Alactic meaning without lactate; you will see why this is important later. For the next eight seconds ATP is rapidly recycled by Creatine

Kinase which hands back a phosphate to the newly formed adenosine diphosphate (tail only has two remaining phosphates) to recycle it back into adenosine triphosphate (a full tail of three phosphates). This can only last for a maximum of approximately ten seconds until stores are depleted enough to reach a threshold. When a threshold is reached it can be thought of like a hybrid car. When one motor has reached its limit then another with a different fuel source must take over.

The next energy system to take over is the lactic acid system. The by-product of this energy system is lactate, hence the name. One molecule of glucose is broken down into pyruvate creating two molecules of ATP in the process. The ATP is turned into energy, as before, and the pyruvate is turned into lactate, AKA lactic acid. This can only last for up to a couple of minutes before we reach the next threshold called the lactate threshold. This is where lactate is at an unsustainable level and intensity must drop significantly if you are to continue moving.

Finally, there is the Aerobic system, which uses oxygen to oxidise carbohydrates, fatty acids and to a lesser extent proteins. This is by far the most efficient energy system. It can maintain exercise intensity for a long duration. Each molecule of glucose produces approximately 38 molecules of ATP, nineteen times the amount of the lactic acid system. One molecule of fatty acid produces over 100 molecules of ATP, just at a much slower rate. When a marathon runner has used up most of their glycogen stores and fatty acids become the main fuel source they slow down drastically. This is known as 'hitting the wall' because that's the feeling you get.

When exercise is increasing in duration the energy system gets shifted right as each energy system fails because of capacity restraints.

Alactic → Lactic Acid → Aerobic

When exercise is increasing in intensity the energy system gets shifted left as energy systems fail to generate energy quick enough.

Aerobic → Lactic Acid → Alactic

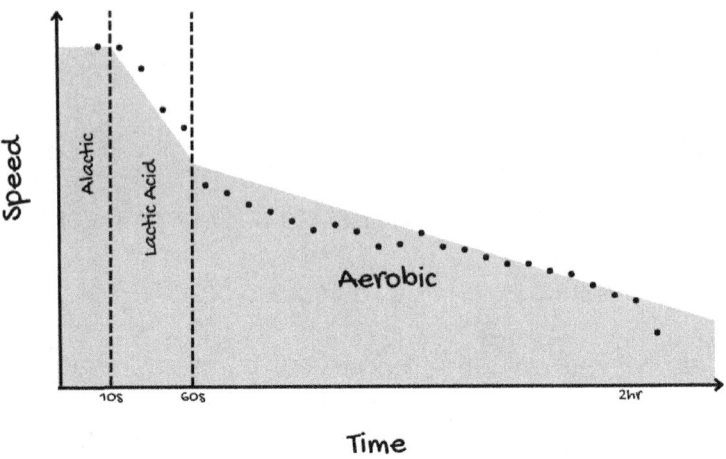

If you want to see the maximum potential of the human body, you just look at the world record holders in the relevant sport. Looking at the world record average speeds in track and road running as of the end of the Paris 2024 Olympics you can see the energy systems in action. We can see that peak output occurs in the 50, 60, 100 and 200 metres with an average speed of nine to ten metres per second. In a study in 2011 Belgian sports scientists recorded Usain Bolt reaching maximum velocity at the 68th metre of a race. A speed of 12.22

metres per second. Between 400m and 800m we can see a threshold is hit. Then the difference in speed between the 800m and the half marathon records is a drop of less than two metres per second. Once an athlete is powering their performance aerobically there is a very gradual decline in speed.

It doesn't perfectly illustrate the difference between the alactic system and the lactic acid system because of the time it takes sprinters to get up to maximum velocity, but it's a great illustration of energy systems past the first minute.

Sports scientists now understand for maximum performance under a minute the limiting factor is maximum force production. This is not the same for maximum performance over a minute. The limiting factor here is being able to sustain those force productions. For example, the marathon world record runner Kelvin Kiptum averages 5.83m/s over 42 kilometres.

Your Alactic system will be conditioning through heavy resistance training where you are generating as maximum force over a very short duration. Your lactic acid system will be conditioned through sets of resistance training that last approximately 60-90 seconds, including your conditioning bouts. Later I will give you the best exercises that will boost your conditioning at the same time as stimulating your muscles. That leaves your aerobic system to train outside of your sessions.

Training your aerobic system is very simple, pick a distance and see how quick you can run it. If you don't want to run you can cycle, or swim, or use any means you want to be able to repeatedly test. Running one kilometre is a perfect start. How fast can you complete a kilometre? Can you beat it over time? Then can you increase the distance and beat the new distance? All the while you are burning calories and improving your endurance.

If we don't lift weights to burn calories, why do we do it? Let's look at that next.

MUSCLE PROTEIN

SYNTHESIS

All muscular contraction and thus movement is powered by a molecule called adenosine triphosphate (ATP). ATP is basically the currency of human movement. ATP is an adenosine molecule with a tail of three phosphates. An enzyme called ATPase breaks off the end phosphate, releasing an explosion of energy that is used to power movement such as a muscular contraction.

We've already discussed protein balance from a nutrition point of view, but that's only half of the equation. You can eat right, and nothing will happen if there's no stimulus, just as much as you can have a stimulus but without the resources for adaptation then nothing changes. So how do we build muscle from training? We know that resistance training builds muscle, but how?

We have already touched on muscle growth being possible when protein synthesis exceeds protein breakdown. An optimal diet not only provides a continual source of resources to build these proteins but creates the environment conducive to muscle building. Think of an optimal diet as delivering the right nutrients like lorries delivering bricks (amino acids) to a building site (muscles). The bricks still need to be made into the new walls.

Assuming you are creating the perfect nutritional environment for muscle building, how do you create the right stimulus for muscle growth? The three factors that take the resources you are delivering to your muscles and turn them into new muscle tissue are: mechanical tension, muscle damage and metabolic stress.

Mechanical Tension

There are two key forces that are exerted on a body by gravity. These are compression and tension. Compression forces are squeezing forces when the force is applied the object will get smaller. If I were to put a book on top of your head the book would be exerting a compressive force on your body. The other force is tension, this is the opposite force to compression, an object will elongate when tensile forces are applied. If I took the book off your head and put it in your outstretched hand the book is now exerting a tensile force on the muscle in your arm and shoulder. Holding a weight down below like you would for a bent over row would be an example of tension. Muscles pull themselves shorter by sliding filaments inside muscle fibres that latch onto each other and rapidly pull the muscle fibres shorter. Muscles cannot be compressed by resistance, but they are tensioned as they pull shorter to resist being lengthened by - or to overcome - an external force i.e., a dumbbell.

Resistance is applied to muscles via a lever. A lever is a rigid bar - a bone - that is rotated around an axis - a joint. This rotational force is called a moment. The bar that the moment is applied to is called the moment arm. Force is applied at 90 degrees to the moment arm to create a rotational force. You already know this intuitively if you have pedalled a bike. You will naturally push the pedal round to three o'clock to apply gravitational force in the most effective way. Pushing down vertically on the pedal at 90 degrees to the horizontal axis of the moment arm of the pedal crank.

When you are lifting weights, as the weight moves further away from the body it may 'feel' heavier. The mass of the weight isn't changing but the force it transfers to the working muscle is multiplied along the length of the moment arm. Gravity always acts vertically down. When a dumbbell is being held in the hand down by your side the centre of mass is directly under the shoulder where the rotation will occur. There is no rotation when the weight is hanging straight down therefore the moment arm equals zero. As the moment arm moves closer to 90 degrees to gravity i.e., horizontally away from the body, the moment increase greatly. For example, when you hold a weight with straight arms either straight out or straight in front of you.

When you are lifting weights, you are manipulating different types of levers.

There are three components to a lever: the force, the axis and the resistance. The resistance is the weight such as a dumbbell or barbell, or just the weight of the body or a limb in body weight exercises. The force is the force that is applied by the working muscle. The axis is the point at which the force and the resistance apply rotational forces around. This is typically the centre of a joint Levers are classified by the position of the three points in relation to each other.

The Paddle (Axis - Force - Resistance)

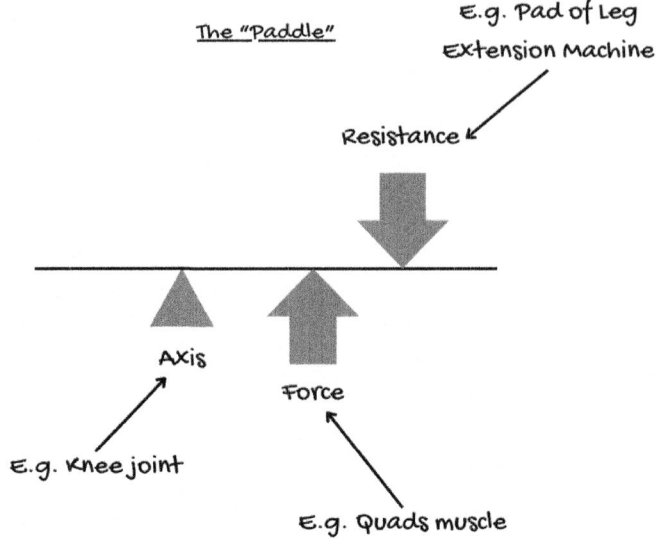

Most joints in the human body are known as "class three levers" but I prefer to call them "the paddle". This type of lever is typically seen in hinge joints like the knee and elbow, or in simple flexion movements. The axis is nearest the centre of the joint. The force is applied close to the axis; muscles attach inside the body and therefore close to the joint. The resistance is applied externally; a weight is held in the hand, or a barbell is held across the back. The force applied is between the axis and the resistance. Think of it like a canoe paddle. The axis that the paddle is rotating around is the hand on the handle at the top of the paddle, trying to keep the top of the paddle relatively still whilst the other hand applies the rowing force in the middle. Pulling back the paddle against the resistance of the water at the bottom end of the paddle. This transfers the force through the stationary hand, the rower's body and the canoe to create propulsion.

In weightlifting terms, think of it like the elbow joint being the axis, the biceps muscles are where the force is applied on the lower arm and the resistance is the force of gravity on the dumbbell being held in the hand.

Force and resistance act in opposite directions and therefore always oppose each other. Either the force is trying to accelerate the object and the resistance is acting as the brakes, or the resistance is accelerating the object and the force being applied is acting as the brakes. In fact both are occurring simultaneously, but one will be overcoming the other. When lifting a free weight, either you are overcoming gravity and lifting it, or you are yielding to gravity and acting as the brake. The most optimal way to create tension is to overcome gravity by accelerating as fast as possible, and by yielding as slowly as possible. This creates an ideal tempo. Faster when lifting, slower when lowering.

The Wheelbarrow (Axis - Resistance - Force)

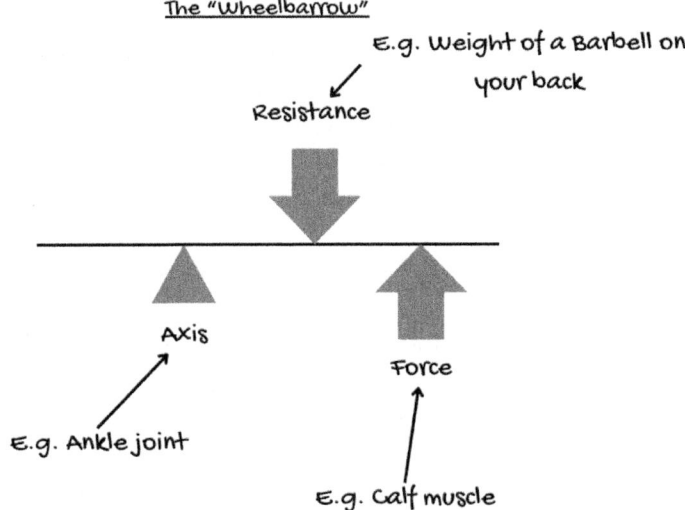

There are very few joints that are this type of lever in the human body. A class two lever is similar to a wheelbarrow where the axis is the wheel, the resistance is the load in the wheelbarrow, and the force is applied by the person lifting the handles. In training, this typically occurs when the axis is a point away from the joint; an example being the ankle during a calf raise. The axis is a point under the ball of the foot, the resistance is the body weight plus any additional load acting down through the mid to rear foot and the force is applied by the calf muscle through the Achilles tendon on the back of the heel.

The Seesaw (Force - Axis - Resistance)

The "See-saw"

Resistance   Force

E.g. Dumbbell   E.g. Triceps muscle
Axis

E.g. Elbow

Finally, there is the seesaw. This is the classic lever, where the resistance is at one end of a lever, like one child on one end of a seesaw. The axis is in the middle, like the balance point of the seesaw. The force is applied at the opposite end, like the other child at the other end of the seesaw. When Archimedes said, "Give me a firm place to stand and a lever and I can move the Earth."

233

This is the lever he was talking about. One example would be in the upper arm when you perform a triceps press. The arm is extended with the resistance being held in the hand. The axis is the centre of the elbow joint. The triceps apply force on the opposite side of the elbow to the resistance to create rotation.

Applying tension to a muscle successfully is like a game of swingball, where you must hit a tennis ball on the end of a length of string. The other end of the string is looped around a corkscrew. Hitting the ball in an arc around the pole will provide enough tension on the string to keep the loop taut around the corkscrew. You transfer tension most effectively when you hit the ball in an arc slightly larger than but as close to the circumference of the circle that the string creates. There's no benefit to hitting the ball across this circle or in any other direction other than around the pole. The take home message from this section is that your goal when stimulating muscles is to create maximal tension. Only when muscles are under tension are they stimulated.

Momentum kills tension as soon as weights are moving inefficiently tension is lost. The "weight" you are lifting is not the full weight of the dumbbell in your hand. Don't lift with your ego, use weights that you can maintain full tension with.

Muscular Damage

Mechanical tension effectively applied to working muscles causes micro trauma to the muscle fibres. The need to repair this damage is a potent signal for muscle protein synthesis. The inflammation caused by these micro traumas to muscle fibres signals to immune cells to remove damage and to repair the muscle. Significantly more damage is caused when the resistance is pulling the muscle and lengthening it under tension. This is known as eccentric loading.

According to the general adaptation syndrome, for the human body to be better prepared for future stress of exercise, muscular damage needs to be repaired back to, or greater than, previous levels. This is done by

Satellite cells. Satellite cells are a type of 'blank' stem cell present in muscle fibre that are turned into mature muscle cells and used to patch up damaged muscle fibres. Supercompensation occurs where the muscle is repaired to a greater degree than before. Muscle strength and size is gradually increased over time by the correct timing of resistance training and recovery.

General Adaptation Syndrome

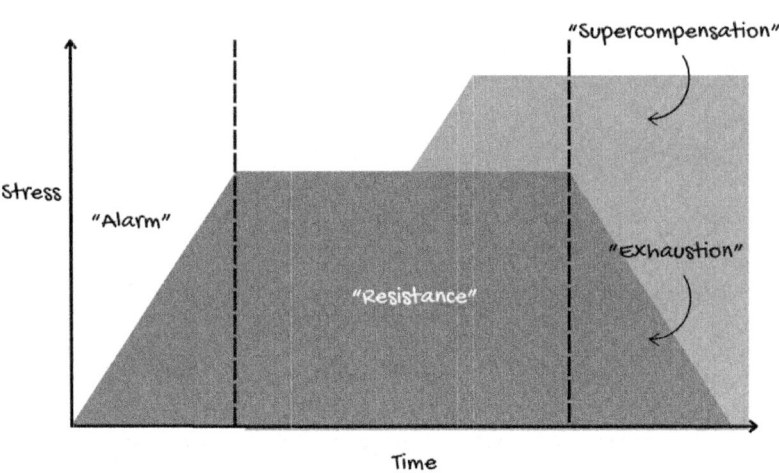

New structural proteins are built out of free amino acids. This is an anabolic process that relies on the right environment within the muscle as mentioned earlier in the nutrition section. If protein synthesis exceeds the protein breakdown to amino acids a positive protein balance will be maintained, and muscle strength and size will increase.

Training should never intentionally set out to create any kind of damage. The damage I am talking about occurs at a microscopic level because of muscular tension. The cells in a muscle fibre are a fraction of the width of a human hair. Effecting microscopic damage is created mainly by a slow and heavy eccentric loading of a muscle. This is controlled through tempo and technique.

Tempo is often referred to using a two-, three- or four-digit code. The two key numbers in tempo are the eccentric and concentric phase of a muscle contraction: a 'repetition'. The eccentric phase as mentioned earlier is when the muscle acts as a brake to slow the weight against the force of gravity acting upon it. The muscle yields to gravity if the weight is lowered. During a concentric contraction a weight is raised against gravity and the weight moves vertically up. The contractile force of the muscle exceeds and overcomes the resistance force of gravity.

To get the most out of the tension created by resistance within a muscle, a fast tempo should be used to overcome the resistance force of gravity by a greater degree. The opposite is true during an eccentric contraction where the muscle is yielding to gravity and is acting as the brake against the acceleration of gravity. You want a brake to slowly let the resistance out. You never want any brake to suddenly switch off. The force acting on the weight is gravity and is a constant. To get the most out of every eccentric contraction the goal is to absorb as much tension as possible from the force of the weight.

The other numbers often cited are the pauses between the eccentric and concentric contraction and again between the concentric and the eccentric contraction. At the bottom and the top of a rep. An eccentric contraction always occurs when a free weight is lowered towards the floor. The opposite is true for a concentric contraction. During a concentric contraction the weight is always moved vertically away from the floor against gravity. Fixed machines and cable machines use weight stacks whereby the weight stack is always being moved against gravity regardless of the directional movement of the cable. The cable could be moving down like in a pull down, but this is translated to raising a weight stack vertically via a system of pulleys.

A target of up to one second of concentric contraction is ideal, whereas an eccentric contraction should be 3-5 times as long. Tempo should be considered in context with the number of repetitions. Fewer repetitions with slower tempo can have the same time under tension as more reps with a quicker tempo. However, more repetitions mean more periods where the tension forces are minimised. This occurs at the top of a squat when the body and legs are straight, and the weight of the bar is primarily being transferred through the spine and bones of the legs. Small activations of the postural muscles are keeping the body balanced. The large muscles in the glutes, quadriceps and hamstrings aren't under tension as such.

Repetitions are not used because we need to clock up a particular number. Repetitions are used to allow for concentric and eccentric activation of a muscle and are repeated so that we can accumulate a certain amount of time whilst the muscle is under tension. Increasing this time under tension increases the metabolic stress on the active muscles. A typical tempo for an exercise will look like this: 3110; this means lowering for a count of three, pause at the bottom of the rep for a second, contract the muscle concentrically for a second and no pause between repetitions. Try this is your workout and you should feel the tension ramp up!

Metabolic Stress

Metabolic stress occurs when an energy deficit is created within a muscle and because of the burning of fuel a build-up of by-products is created. This energy deficit, the build-up of metabolic by-products and changes in the pH of the muscle signal to the rest of the body that stress is occurring, and the body responds. The muscle cells swell up because of the build-up of by-products and the increased supply of nutrients and fluid to the muscle cells. This signals enzymes such as insulin-like growth factor (IGF-1) which stimulates protein synthesis.

It is the response to metabolic stress that stimulates increased muscle strength and size. The human body is always striving for homeostatic balance. Any disturbance to this balance stimulates adaptation to lessen the effects of the disruption in the future. A progressive training plan keeps moving the goalposts by just the right amount to keep an onward progression as effectively as possible. Intensity plays a large part in metabolic stress being a factor of muscle protein synthesis but relative to rest times. Rest times between working sets allow the flushing of some of these by-products before the next set. An appropriate rest interval allows some recovery to keep the intensity of the workout up but not so much so that a lot of the metabolic stress is dissipated, and the resulting signal is weakened.

Rest times

Rest time is all the time that muscles aren't under tension within a training session, from the first working set to the last. This includes time taken to change weights, drink water etc. The more time spent resting the greater the working muscles are allowed to return to their resting state, but rest too long and the training stimulus is dissipated. The time muscles spend under tension relative to the total workout time is the training density. The more time within the session spent under tension the greater the training density. Yes, just like food has energy density; working out has training density. The greater the training density the greater the metabolic stress!

An effective training plan acknowledges the role of mechanical tension, muscular damage and metabolic stress and plans to utilise these three components to maximise positive muscle protein synthesis. Using a range of intensities, rep ranges, volumes and tempos will create the maximum stimuli possible. The careful management of intensity with volume and tempo will produce the best results. Not forsaking one for the others. Often the case is intensity is prioritised at the expense of tempo. We will discuss these in further detail in the next section.

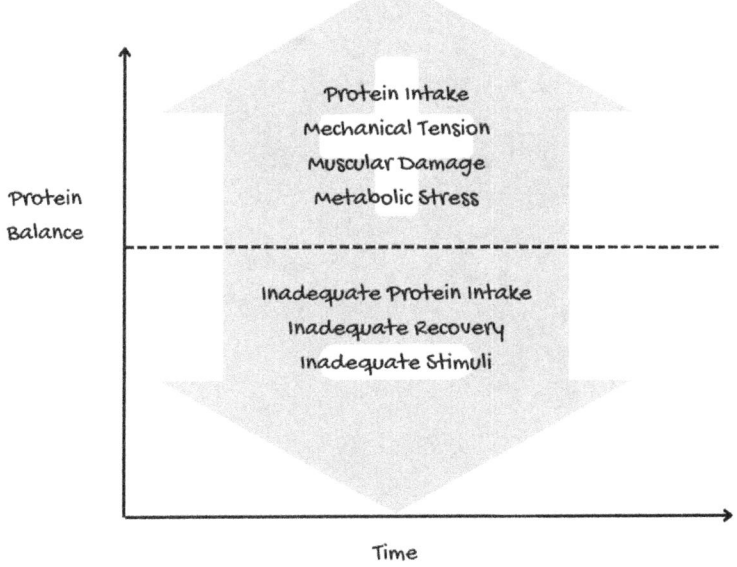

Next, we'll look at exactly how to manage training volume and intensity to make progress from session to session.

MAKING PROGRESS

Milo of Croton was a six-time Olympic champion in the

6th century BCE. A famous wrestler, his training started

at an early age. Milo had a pet calf, and he carried that

calf on his shoulder every day. The average calf weighs

between 60 and 90 pounds at birth and then will double

its birth weight by the time it's 60 days old. Then until it

reaches its adult weight, around its second birthday, the

calf will gain about two pounds per day. This means Milo

was lifting a 60–90-pound weight and incrementally

increasing the weight every day by one to two pounds.

Milo went on to become one of the greatest wrestlers of

ancient Greece. This story is used as the metaphor for

what we now call 'progressive overload'; incrementally increasing the load over time.

Remember the story about John Naber the Olympic swimmer who broke down his goal over four years to win gold and set a world record? Most people overlook the power of setting goals beyond the original goal such as the total amount of weight they want to lose. This is because of the lack of clarity around what the goals mean to the overall goal. You don't have to be able to squat or bench a certain weight to be the shape you want to be. But this is the beauty of goal setting where the process is not directly linked to the outcome, that improvement happens at every level. You and I will lift completely different weights for every exercise. But what we can lift does not dictate our outcome, the fact that we both individually increase what we are doing week on week will ensure progress. The things we discussed earlier; protein synthesis and fat oxidation are largely a by-product of not only what we do but what we improve on when exercising.

There are two things that you can increase to keep improving your body composition: volume and intensity. Volume is the number of sets of an exercise. Whether it be cardio, conditioning, or resistance exercises. A single set is a single bout or dose of exercise. You can count either the total number of sets you do or the number of sets you do per exercise or per muscle group. This tells you how many doses you have per session and per week. Intensity is how high the work you are doing is relative to a maximum. This is often compared to the maximum weight you can lift during resistance training for a given exercise, or your theoretical heart rate maximum during conditioning.

Frequency isn't a metric for progress because you can only increase frequency once or twice. If you start at an optimal frequency, which once we've created your programme you will have then there is nowhere for you to increase frequency to. If you were to change from a whole-body programme to a split body programme, the frequency of each of your muscle groups will decrease because you are changing from training each muscle group every session to every other session. Likewise, changing the exercise won't progress your body composition *per se*, rather it just changes the mode by which you can then start to increase volume and intensity again. That is if you master a dumbbell bench press until you are struggling to make progress in weight or reps and plateau, so you switch to a barbell bench press. Changing the exercise won't give you more progress from session one, but you will be able to now master another exercise for the same muscles and start to increase volume and intensity again. It is these increases in volume and intensity that will give you the strength and body composition changes.

Sometimes it is difficult to see when progress is being made. Later I will teach you how to assess your strength and how this can be turned into a useful tool that will show you if you are making progress or not. Here's what your typical progress might look like in one exercise:

Exercise	Sets	Reps	Weight
Dumbbell Bench Press	3	10	25
Dumbbell Bench Press	3	10	30
Dumbbell Bench Press	3	12	30
Dumbbell Bench Press	3	8	35
Dumbbell Bench Press	4	9	35

Minimal Dose and Diminishing Returns

There is what is known as a 'dose response' to training. The results you get are correlated to the amount of work you do up to a point. To get results you must hit the minimum threshold. The good news is for beginners this is as low as one session per week, with weights approximately half as heavy as maximum, and only three sets per movement. As you become more experienced this threshold gradually increases as time goes by. If you imagine at the other end of the spectrum, you have world-class athletes who are putting everything in terms of training, nutrition, sleep, technology etc. to eke out the most marginal gain possible. Diminishing returns means that for the same amount of effort you will yield gradually less and less results over time. If you are doing the same from week to week you will be going backwards because your body is lacking the fresh progressive stimulus it requires to stimulate growth.

You have already calculated your genetic potential as your fat-free mass index (FFMI) and have a rough idea of how much of your potential you have capitalised.

Let's discuss how to purposefully make progress looking more specifically at intensity and volume. Volume is simply how many times you do a particular exercise; intensity is the proportional magnitude of the exercise. Tracking both are key to understanding how much you are doing within and between training sessions. There is a negative linear relationship between intensity and volume. As you increase the intensity of your training the volume you do has to yield. The good news is for beginners or those returning from a long break from training, for a while you will be able to make linear progression and be able to increase both volume and

intensity at the same time.

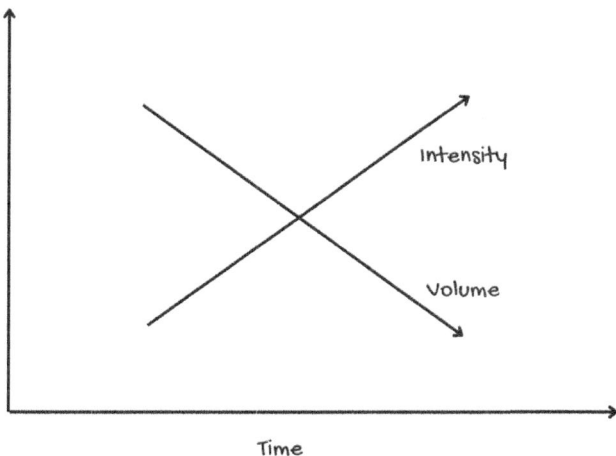

First let's look at intensity in detail.

INTENSITY

Simply put, intensity is the magnitude of the weight you are lifting. The force of the weight is determined by its mass in kilograms and the acceleration of gravity which is a constant $9.81m/s^2$. Gravity only moves on one axis (direction), vertically down. The only efficient path to moving a weight against gravity is vertically up. As the acceleration of gravity is constant, as the mass of the weight increases so too does the vertical force acting on the weight. The greater the weight, the greater the amount of force that will generate more tension within the working muscle. A weight of one kilogram accelerating at one metre per second per second will produce a force of one Newton (N). The function of skeletal muscle is to generate force. Force is the ability to accelerate mass.

$$Force\ (N) = Mass\ (kg) \times Acceleration\ \left(\frac{m}{s^2}\right)$$

If you maintain the same tempo on a specific exercise, by increasing the weight you also increase the force proportionally. A ten-kilogram dumbbell being acted upon by gravity will produce a force of 98.1N. You will have to apply more force to the dumbbell than this to overcome gravity. If you equal 98.1N of force, then the dumbbell will stay exactly where it is as the two forces are equalled and cancelled out. As soon as you apply any more than 98.1N on the dumbbell it will start to move vertically up. As the acceleration of a free weight cannot be altered, we alter the mass to increase the amount of force required to move it. Increasing the weight, increases the force and therefore increases what we call the intensity. To stress the muscles in a progressive way is to train them to lift progressively more mass, creating more force and more intensity over time. This will stimulate the working muscle to a greater degree each time. In the chapter 'Measuring

Strength' I will show you how to measure relative intensity. Just think of intensity linearly; increasing weight equals increasing intensity. The goal of resistance training is to lift more weights and increase intensity over time.

The first goal of resistance training is increasing intensity for each exercise. If you lifted ten kilograms one week, lift more than ten kilograms the next week. If you squat 60 kilograms, next week try and squat 65 kilograms. This is the most obvious example of overload, adding more weight. A step up from 50kg to 60kg is a 20% increase in intensity. The first plateau people experience in their training is because they stop increasing their weights and stop increasing the intensity. Settling on the same weights = plateauing.

You must balance intensity with volume, otherwise you would just keep lifting your maximum weight for a single every time you trained. Altering the volume is a good way to change the stimulus when you can't simply increase the weight.

Let's look at volume next.

VOLUME

Volume can be split into two parts; intra-set volume, which is the number of repetitions and inter-set volume which is the number of sets. There is an inverse linear relationship between the intraset volume and the intensity of a resistance exercise. As intensity increases volume decreases. This is the graphic of volume and intensity you saw a few pages ago. If you successfully complete ten repetitions, then increase that weight continually, eventually you will reach a weight that you can only complete one repetition with. Increase it further and you will find a weight that you cannot execute even one repetition with. A moderate volume is the trade-off between a high and low intensity.

A very basic rule of thumb is that as volume increases from one repetition to two repetitions the intensity drops by approximately 5%. Then 5% for every increase of two repetitions thereafter. Four repetitions can be completed at 90% of 1RM, six repetitions at 85% and so on. There are exceptions depending on ability and muscle fibre make up. Elite endurance athletes can contradict this rule and perform more repetitions at lower intensities.

Increased muscle strength and size can be stimulated at a variety of repetition ranges. All rep ranges contribute to mechanical tension, muscle damage and metabolic stress. Higher intensities will produce more intense stimuli but over a shorter duration. Lower intensities will create stimuli that are less intense but over longer durations.

The best approach is a two-pronged attack utilising intensity and volume. Aim to increase intensity first. If you cannot increase intensity and maintain technique and tension, then keep the same intensity but increase volume. Initially by increasing the number of repetitions, and then when you can't increase the number of repetitions increase the number of sets. It is easier to increase the number of sets rather than the number of repetitions because of the added rest interval between efforts. If you increase the number of repetitions for the same weight, you will still be increasing your strength until the point where you can increase the weight. This toing and froing of weight and repetitions is how you make progress over time. Increase weight, if you can't then increase reps until the point where you can increase the weight.

Exercise	Sets	Reps	Weight
Dumbbell Bench Press	3	10	25
Dumbbell Bench Press	3	10	30
Dumbbell Bench Press	3	7	35
Dumbbell Bench Press	3	8	35
Dumbbell Bench Press	3	9	35
Dumbbell Bench Press	3	9	35
Dumbbell Bench Press	3	10	35
Dumbbell Bench Press	3	8	40
Dumbbell Bench Press	3	8	40

Increase the weight for the same repetitions until you can't manage the same number of repetitions. Then aim to get the number of repetitions up to the previous level but with the new weight. If you can, then try to increase the weight again and repeat the process. If you can't then add more sets to get more volume in at that weight.

Now you know how we're going to apply the loading patterns we now need to understand what muscles we are going to apply them to.

MUSCLE GROUPS

There are over 600 named muscles in the human body. It is much simpler to think of these muscles in terms of 'groups' of muscles that perform similar movements. Exercises can also be described as movements and associated muscles that create that movement.

For the human body to work as a unified system most of these muscles overlap, performing multiple movements across multiple joints. For example, the hamstrings are a group of three major muscles: the biceps femoris, the semimembranosus and semitendinosus muscles. The hamstrings attach to the back of the tibia (shin bone) and the hip and the femur. They flex the knee as well as straighten the hip. This interaction creates more complex movements by holding one of these joints still whilst the other moves. For simplicity I will refer to exercises by their movement and indicate the major muscles that contribute to that movement.

If we take the total of these muscles and divide them into the main movement patterns you can split the body into upper and lower compartments. Upper body concerns muscles that mobilise the shoulders and elbows and the lower body concerns muscles that mobilise the hips, knees, and ankles. Now we have the following:

Upper body: horizontal press (using the pecs and anterior (front) deltoids), horizontal row (using the latissimus dorsi, rhomboids and rear deltoids of the back), vertical press (using the anterior deltoids and the medial (middle) deltoids), vertical row (using the latissimus dorsi), elbow flexion (using the biceps) and elbow extension (using the triceps). Lower body: Hip extension (using the gluteals and hamstrings), knee flexion (using the hamstrings), knee extension (using the quadriceps), ankle plantarflexion (using the calves) and trunk flexion and extension (using the rectus abdominis (abdominals) and erectors (lower back).

A basic understanding of anatomy will help you greatly with your training. You don't have to become a physiologist; I have given you enough to get started. Understanding what movements are created by what muscles and how to increase tension will improve your results drastically.

Muscles work as chains, typically most muscles will cross more than one joint. Some movements occurring in multiple exercises; The elbow is flexed during horizontal pulling and vertical pulling. Elbows are extended (straightened) during horizontal pressing and vertical pressing. You will be using your pecs during a bench press, and your deltoids during a shoulder press, and both will stimulate the triceps to straighten the elbow. These exercises are known as compound exercises because they mobilise multiple joints simultaneously.

The upper body is also more complex than the lower body, simply because you cannot orient your lower body in space like you can orient your upper body. There are prone (face down) exercises where you work the muscles in your posterior (back) and supine (face up) exercises where you work the muscles in your anterior (front). Bar a leg extension and leg curl machine most lower body exercises are done standing and therefore are typically either a squat pattern or deadlift pattern. Both of which place a different emphasis on the anterior and posterior chains of muscles.

As the 600 muscles in the body can be grouped into twelve movement patterns, six upper body and six lower body, I will refer to movement patterns when discussing exercises. Let's transfer these movement patterns into a programme. An effective programme depends on how many times per week you will commit to training. This will dictate how your training is split.

Let's look at your options for training frequency next.

TRAINING SPLITS

In this chapter we will use your weekly sessions to decide on your training splits. The more sessions you want to do, the further you will split your training. Each muscle group needs to be stimulated every 3-4 days. Your training will be split so that you can train each muscle group twice per week.

If you can only commit to three training sessions per week, then it makes sense to train your whole body each session. Any less and you will miss the required frequency. If you are training four to five times per week then you take all the movements and divide them into two groups. You have two splits that you can train each twice per week giving you your four sessions. The easiest way to do this is alluded to above and that is to split the body into upper and lower body. Of course, you can split the muscle groups any way you like. If it makes sense to you. To progress further you would further subdivide all the muscle groups into three groups. Train each group twice a week giving you six sessions per week. With seven days in a week, it is not possible to further divide beyond this unless you want to dedicate your life to training and train more than once per day. There are years of mileage in training three, four and six times a week before you even need to consider training a second session a day.

It is important to remember that the spacing of training days is less important than the number of training sessions completed[13]. Remember this when you lose a training day to other commitments. A lot of the time life will get in the way!

---

[13] Yang, Y., Bay, P. B., Wang, Y. R., Huang, J., Teo, H. W. J., & Goh, J. (2018). Effects of Consecutive Versus Non-consecutive Days of Resistance Training on Strength, Body Composition, and Red Blood Cells. Frontiers in physiology, 9, 725. https://doi.org/10.3389/fphys.2018.00725

Let's look at a two-to-three-day routine first.

Up to three times per week

An efficient whole-body routine utilises compound exercises. These are exercises that use multiple muscles over multiple joints. By using compound exercises you are using the 'crossover effect' to your advantage. The same muscles are used across multiple exercises. Rather than isolating individual muscles and training them in series, you are training the assisting muscles in tandem with larger muscles. If you bench press and overhead press, you are working your anterior deltoids and pecs on the bench press and medial deltoids on the overhead press and stimulating your triceps in both exercises. This allows you to drop the triceps exercise from your whole-body routine. Elbow flexion and extension exercises will be stimulated during the other compound upper body exercises. The movements of the lower body can be grouped into two large movement patterns. The lower body uses the three main joints: the hip, knee, and ankle simultaneously. These happen in a squat movement and a hip hinge movement. In the energy systems chapter, I explained why conditioning is important in every session. I have added a conditioning exercise to increase the cardiovascular intensity. This gives you a list of nine exercises to complete during a session.

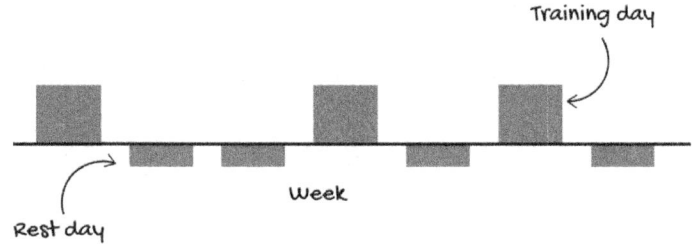

When your training frequency is limited a 'circuit' style training approach is optimal. You can keep the intensity of the sessions high by working through rounds of all nine exercises. I start all my clients on a three times per week whole body routine to get a baseline on all the different movement patterns. It will also give you the greatest bang-for-buck in terms of future progression. You progress the volume and intensity of all the movement patterns linearly. When you want to make the biggest shift in your training you can step up to the next level for training frequency; four or more sessions per week.

Movement Pattern	Exercise examples	Major muscle groups worked
Squat	Barbell Squat, Goblet Squat, Split Squat	Quadriceps, Glutes, Hamstrings.
Hip hinge	Romanian Deadlift, Good Morning, Glute Bridge	Glutes, Hamstrings
Horizontal Press	Dumbbell/Barbell Bench Press, Incline Press	Pecs, Anterior Deltoids, Triceps
Horizontal Pull	Barbell/Dumbbell Row, Seal Row, Single Arm Row	Latissimus Dorsi, Rhomboids, Rear Deltoids, Biceps
Vertical Press	Dumbbell/Barbell Overhead Press either Seated/Standing	Medial/Anterior Deltoids, Triceps
Vertical Pull	Pull ups, Chin ups, Pull Downs	Latissimus Dorsi, Rhomboids, Rear Deltoids, Biceps
Calf Raises	Barbell/Dumbbell Single/Double Calf Raises	Gastrocnemius, Soleus
Trunk	Plank, Rollout, Weighted Full Sit ups, Back Hyperextension	Rectus Abdominis, Erectors, Hip Flexors, Transverse Abdominis
Conditioning	Sprint on any cardio machine/ergometer	Cardiovascular, Anaerobic system

Movement Pattern	Exercise	Major muscle groups worked	Sets	Reps	Rest
Squat	Barbell Squat	Quadriceps, Glutes, Hamstrings.	3	15	Minimal
Hip hinge	Romanian Deadlift	Glutes, Hamstrings	3	15	60-180s
Horizontal Press	Dumbbell Bench Press	Pecs, Anterior Deltoids, Triceps	3	15	Minimal
Horizontal Pull	Barbell Row	Latissimus Dorsi, Rhomboids, Rear Deltoids, Biceps	3	15	Minimal
Vertical Press	Dumbbell Overhead Press Seated	Medial/Anterior Deltoids, Triceps	3	15	Minimal
Vertical Pull	Pull ups	Latissimus Dorsi, Rhomboids, Rear Deltoids, Biceps	3	15	Minimal
Calf Raises	Barbell Single Calf Raises	Gastrocnemius, Soleus	3	15	Minimal
Trunk	Plank	Rectus Abdominis, Erectors, Hip Flexors, Transverse Abdominis	3	Max Time	Minimal
Conditioning	Rower Sprint	Cardiovascular, Anaerobic system	3	60s	Minimal

Four times per week

To increase the frequency more than three times per week, you must split your movement patterns into two groups. This is known as a split body routine. You split the whole-body routine into two halves. The simplest and most logical split is upper body and lower body. Still training each movement pattern twice a week gives you a total of four sessions per week.

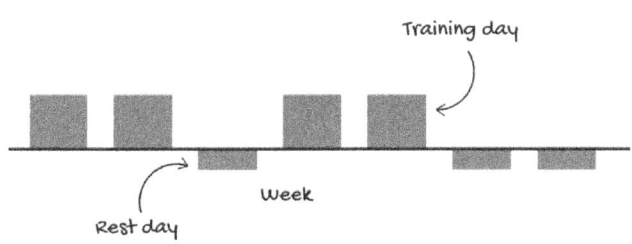

Now you have room to add in isolation exercises. Isolating the quadriceps with knee extension exercises, the hamstrings with knee flexion exercises, the biceps with elbow flexion exercises and the triceps with elbow extension exercises. Now is a good time to add in some shoulder extension as an insurance policy to keep the shoulders healthy to counteract the pressing you are doing. This is added with some simple reverse flyes.

Movement Pattern	Exercise examples	Major muscle groups worked
Squat	Barbell Squat, Goblet Squat, Split Squat	Quadriceps, Glutes, Hamstrings.
Hip hinge	Romanian Deadlift, Good Morning, Glute Bridge	Glutes, Hamstrings
Knee Extension	Leg Extension Machine	Quadriceps
Knee Flexion	Hamstring Curl Machine	Hamstrings
Calf Raises	Barbell/Dumbbell Single/Double Calf Raises	Gastrocnemius, Soleus
Trunk	Plank, Rollout, Weighted Full Sit ups, Back Hyperextension	Rectus Abdominis, Erectors, Hip Flexors, Transverse Abdominis
Conditioning	Sprint on any cardio machine/ergometer	Cardiovascular, Anaerobic system

Movement Pattern	Exercise examples	Major muscle groups worked
Horizontal Press	Dumbbell/Barbell Bench Press, Incline Press	Pecs, Anterior Deltoids, Triceps
Horizontal Pull	Barbell/Dumbbell Row, Seal Row, Single Arm Row	Latissimus Dorsi, Rhomboids, Rear Deltoids, Biceps
Vertical Press	Dumbbell/Barbell Overhead Press either Seated/Standing	Medial/Anterior Deltoids, Triceps
Vertical Pull	Pull ups, Chin ups, Pull Downs	Latissimus Dorsi, Rhomboids, Rear Deltoids, Biceps
Elbow Flexion	Barbell/Dumbbell Biceps Curls	Biceps
Elbow Extension	Barbell/Dumbbell Triceps Extensions	Triceps
Rear Deltoids	Rear deltoid flyes	Posterior Deltoids

This is a typical program I will give to a client and has the optimal balance between volume and frequency. I now need to introduce the different loading patterns. The whole-body routine could be completed as single sets of exercises completing each exercise fully before moving to the next. Or as a circuit where you complete one set of each exercise before repeating as rounds. Now you can group exercises together or train them on their own. This is determined by how taxing each exercise is. The large compound exercises can be completed on their own. The smaller isolation exercises can be completed in pairs; known as 'supersets', or threes; known as 'giant sets'. A letter in the 'Order' column means you complete all sets of that letter before moving to the next, for example all of A before moving onto B and so on. A number means you complete one set of each before repeating until all sets have been completed, such as C1 and C2.

Here's what a program should look like:

Movement	Order	Exercise	Major muscles	Sets	Reps	Rest
Squat	A1	Barbell Squat, Goblet Squat, Split Squat	Quadriceps, Glutes, Hamstrings.	3	8	Minimal
Hip hinge	B1	Romanian Deadlift, Good Morning, Glute Bridge	Glutes, Hamstrings	3	8	60-180s
Knee Extension	C1	Leg Extension Machine	Quadriceps	3	12	Minimal
Knee Flexion	C2	Hamstring Curl Machine	Hamstrings	3	12	Minimal
Calf Raises	D1	Barbell/Dumbbell Single/Double Calf Raises	Gastrocnemius, Soleus	3	15	Minimal
Trunk	D2	Plank, Rollout, Weighted Sit ups, Back Hyperextension	Rectus Abdominis, Erectors, Hip Flexors, Transverse Abdominis	3	15	Minimal
Conditioning	D3	Sprint on any cardio machine	Cardiovascular, Anaerobic system	3	60s	60-180s

Moveme nt	Orde r	Exercise	Major muscles	Set s	Rep s	Rest
Horizontal Press	A1	Dumbbell/Barb ell Bench Press, Incline Press	Pecs, Anterior Deltoids, Triceps	3	8	Minim al
Horizontal Pull	B1	Barbell/Dumbb ell Row, Seal Row, Single Arm Row	Latissimus Dorsi, Rhomboids, Rear Deltoids, Biceps	3	8	60- 180s
Vertical Press	C1	Dumbbell/Barb ell Overhead Press either Seated/Standin g	Medial/Anteri or Deltoids, Triceps	3	12	Minim al
Vertical Pull	C2	Pull ups, Chin ups, Pull Downs	Latissimus Dorsi, Rhomboids, Rear Deltoids, Biceps	3	12	Minim al
Elbow Flexion	D1	Barbell/Dumbb ell Biceps Curls	Biceps	3	15	Minim al
Elbow Extension	D2	Barbell/Dumbb ell Triceps Extensions	Triceps	3	15	Minim al
Rear Deltoids	D3	Rear deltoid flyes	Posterior Deltoids	3	15	60- 180s

Six times per week

You can split your training further. Six times per week is the maximum frequency you can train at without either skipping a rest day or by training more than once per day. Which is ok if you are a professional bodybuilder but for everyone else, let's cap training at 6 sessions per week.

For six sessions per week, you can further split the movement patterns. The easiest way to split further is to separate the pushing and pulling movements. So now the training looks like: pressing, pulling and legs. The shoulder joint is multidirectional, you can extend and flex the shoulder in two directions. The legs you can extend and flex in one direction we can more easily further divide the upper body from our upper and lower body split. You could split the upper body into horizontal and vertical. I tend to do this if joint imbalance is an issue and I want to pair a pressing movement with a pulling movement to keep them in sync. Many people, coaches included, will argue over the perfect split. How you split your training doesn't matter, it's a means to achieve the overall goal of training your every muscle group twice per week. Below

is how a split would look if you were to split your training

into lower, upper push and upper pull.

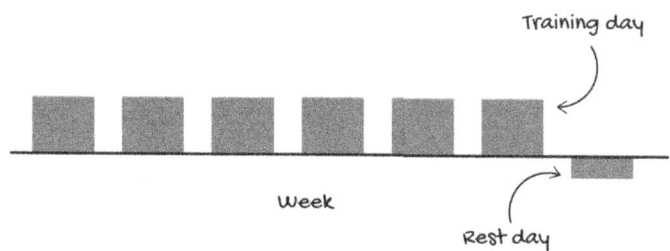

Movement Pattern	Exercise examples	Major muscle groups worked
Squat	Barbell Squat, Goblet Squat, Split Squat	Quadriceps, Glutes, Hamstrings.
Hip hinge	Romanian Deadlift, Good Morning, Glute Bridge	Glutes, Hamstrings
Knee Extension	Leg Extension Machine	Quadriceps
Knee Flexion	Hamstring Curl Machine	Hamstrings
Calf Raises	Barbell/Dumbbell Single/Double Calf Raises	Gastrocnemius, Soleus
Trunk	Plank, Rollout, Weighted Full Sit ups, Back Hyperextension	Rectus Abdominis, Erectors, Hip Flexors, Transverse Abdominis
Conditioning	Sprint on any cardio machine/ergometer	Cardiovascular, Anaerobic system

Movement Pattern	Exercise examples	Major muscle groups worked
Horizontal Press	Dumbbell/Barbell Bench Press, Incline Press	Pecs, Anterior Deltoids, Triceps
Vertical Press	Dumbbell/Barbell Overhead Press either Seated/Standing	Medial/Anterior Deltoids, Triceps
Elbow Extension	Dumbbell/Barbell/Cable Triceps Extensions	Triceps
Pec Flyes	Dumbbell Flyes, Cable Flyes	Pecs, Anterior Deltoid

Movement Pattern	Exercise examples	Major muscle groups worked
Horizontal Pull	Barbell/Dumbbell Row, Seal Row, Single Arm Row	Latissimus Dorsi, Rhomboids, Rear Deltoids, Biceps
Vertical Pull	Pull ups, Chin ups, Pull Downs	Latissimus Dorsi, Rhomboids, Rear Deltoids, Biceps
Elbow Flexion	Dumbbell/Barbell/Cable Bicep Curls	Biceps
Rear Deltoids	Dumbbell/Cable Rear Delt Flyes	Posterior Deltoids

Now you can add in some long lever isolation exercises such as pec flyes and lateral raises. I still alternate the emphasis on either horizontal or vertical on each of the two specific sessions per week. Starting with horizontal one week and vertical the next.

The sessions become smaller but more intense, don't jump in at this split until you have gotten everything you can out of the previous splits. You can increase the volume by repeating movement patterns with different variations of exercises. For example, barbell bench press followed by dumbbell bench press. Keep the balance between movement patterns the same.

Next let's look at the movement patterns and more specifically the exercises that make up the programs.

MOVEMENT PATTERNS

Before we get into the movement patterns of the program, I want to take a brief minute to clarify a few points of safety that are universal when lifting weights. Weight training is one of the safest sports there is. To put it into perspective, an article in the journal *Environmental Research and Public Health* found that weight training averaged 1.12 injuries for every 1,000 hours of training and competition[14]. The injury rate in soccer was over six times as high. That said I still don't want you to hurt

---

[14] Prieto-González, P., Martínez-Castillo, J. L., Fernández-Galván, L. M., Casado, A., Soporki, S., & Sánchez-Infante, J. (2021). Epidemiology of Sports-Related Injuries and Associated Risk Factors in Adolescent Athletes: An Injury Surveillance. International journal of environmental research and public health, 18(9), 4857. https://doi.org/10.3390/ijerph18094857

yourself, because not only is that time out of training but it might put you off.

Dumbbells first

Dumbbells are safer than barbells because you are unlikely to get trapped if you fail a rep. A barbell can pin you, so too can some machines. Start off with dumbbells and if you ever have any doubts about your own safety then seek guidance from a qualified individual.

Barbells

Barbells are still safe, there are two points where injury can occur; either when you fail a repetition or when re-racking your barbell in a rack. When using a barbell, particularly a 7-foot Olympic barbell, get someone you trust and deem competent to spot you. If you can't get a spotter you trust then swap for dumbbells. Alternatively, use spotting arms that attach to the rack or bench you are using, set at a height where you are confident that you can ditch the bar safely. If this reduces the range of the exercise you are doing by a couple of inches, then so

be it. Set the pins just above your chest when bench

pressing or shoulder pressing. If you are squatting, set

the pins an inch below the bottom of your squat. If you

fail your squat, keep your hands well away from the

impact zone of the barbell and the pins and simply tip the

barbell off your back and onto the pins. The barbell

should never have more than an inch or two to drop. This

creates a 'safety zone' which is an imaginary box that you

can drop into when the safety arms catch the barbell.

The easiest way to unrack a barbell is with the barbell

set up in a rack at chest height. You will have to squat it

out of the rack a couple of inches. Being able to drop the

barbell into the rack a couple of inches is much safer than

having to re-rack it on tiptoes. Never re-rack a barbell on

tiptoes. Always aim for the uprights of the rack above the

hooks, never aim for the hooks themselves. You can

miss the hooks if you aim for them, aim above them and

you can't miss. When taking your weights off a barbell

never leave more than a 25-kilogram difference between

sides of the barbell. Never, never fully unload one side leaving weights on the other side. Not unless you want to see how a mediaeval trebuchet works!

Comfort

Do and wear whatever you want to make yourself comfortable in the gym. This is your training, and you need to feel comfortable. Most gym-goers are proud of their shared space. Don't do anything to make anyone else uncomfortable, we're all here for the same reason! Solid footwear in a weights room is better than cushioned running shoes. Just like moist feet, moist hands can and will blister. Chalk the palms for your hands to reduce calluses.

Warming up

You should warm up on every new movement pattern. This can mean warming up on every single exercise in a whole-body program! Warming up doesn't just mean body temperature. On a hot day, telling your coach you're already warm is like when your neighbour tells you to can wash their car after you've finished washing yours. 'Warm up' is just a term for movement preparation. You need to be ready to lift more than you did last session. This section is about how to get yourself ready to do just that.

A warm-up will include some mobility if range is a problem with that movement pattern; hip range of movement on a squat and shoulder range of movement on a bench press are two typical examples. I will give you some mobility exercises for each movement pattern if they are required. Then you complete warm up sets before you complete your work sets. For beginners a warm-up set typically starts with an empty bar and then you add weights progressively until you find your working weight. Once you are more comfortable with your working weights, rather than starting with a 20-kilogram barbell each time, you can start at a percentage - say 50% - and work your way up in increments that feel right to you. Too many warm-up sets will tire you unnecessarily, too few and you won't feel ready to go come your first work set. Find a balance between the two. Depending on the exercise I typically do two to four warm up sets. When you repeat a movement pattern there is no need to warm up again.

Squat

The first of the two main lower body lifts we include in a program is the squat. For a detailed understanding of squat mechanics, I highly recommend reading Starting Strength: Basic Barbell Training by Mark Rippertoe. This is where I got my most detailed understanding of the squat with over 70 pages dedicated solely to this lift alone!

Most people cannot squat with good mechanics. The squat is a skill that takes time to master, don't be disappointed if you feel like you can't get it straight away. I will cover a few key points here, namely where you contact the floor i.e., your foot position and where you contact the bar; your shoulder position. Everything in between should slot itself into the correct position.

Correct foot position starts with the correct width, shoulder width. This gets the thighs out the way of the trunk so that you can squat to a proper depth without your thighs squashing your abdomen. This discomfort stops a lot of people from squatting to a correct depth. If you struggle to squat to full depth because you feel your heels lifting, then you can raise your heels by an inch to simulate more flexible ankles. As well as heel position, the correct position of the toes will also clear space for the torso by the hips. Rotating the toes out to 30 degrees will make way for the torso.

The hands should be as narrow as comfortably possible, always within the thin marks in the grip of a seven-foot Olympic bar. Keep your thumbs positioned over the bar to keep the wrists straight and not take the weight of the bar. The bar should sit just below the spine of the shoulder blade, which you will feel as a bony lump of the shoulder blade. This may feel low, but it helps maintain the centre of mass of the bar over the midfoot. Leading to a much more efficient squat. A more efficient squat means more of the force is going to tension the muscles more effectively. Do not adopt a high bar position where the bar sits up by the cervical vertebrae of the neck. This will give you a slightly more forward lean but will allow the hips a greater degree of flexion.

The best squat exercises are a barbell back squat, goblet squat and split squat. The barbell back squat is the classic squat. The goblet squat is a variation where you hold a dumbbell on your chest, this forces you to keep your torso more vertical. The split squat is where you split your stance which means your knees and hips flex less than in a back squat. Pick one and work on mastering it. As you master the technique you will be able to progress the weight you use. Then you can rotate the exercises and build a repertoire.

Most people become unstuck with their squat because of poor hip mobility. Start with a pigeon stretch. Lie on your front with one leg across and underneath your torso.

Progress into a gorilla stretch; squat as low as you can maintaining a straight trunk, sitting on your heels using the upright of a squat rack to hold onto for support.

The squat is one of two major lower body lifts. Let's look at the hip hinge next.

Hip Hinge

To gain extra stimulation of the hamstrings - as a squat movement pattern places most of its emphasis on the quadriceps and glutes - you can perform a movement known as a hip hinge. It is named a 'hip hinge' because you maintain a solid trunk and relatively straight legs and the movement is isolated to a hinge of the hips. A Romanian deadlift - where the barbell is hanging below the shoulders in the hands - and a good morning - when the barbell is placed across the back - are two examples of a hip hinge. The goal is to keep the feet hip width apart, toes pointing forwards, keep the chest turned upwards and press the backside backwards as if closing a door behind you. This emphasises a movement straight back rather than up or down. Keeping the knee relatively straight will fix the bottom end of the hamstrings and the flexion of the hip will stretch the top end of the hamstrings. The hamstrings cross over the knee and hip joint so don't worry if you struggle with this movement to start. Controlling both joints as the hamstrings lengthen and shorten is hard, but worth mastering.

Where most people come unstuck is their trunk starts to flex when they perform a hip hinge. A flexing trunk slackens hamstrings. Reducing tension in the hamstrings. The goal is to maintain extension of the lower back. To practice this, perform some prone cobras beforehand. Lie on the floor on your front. Peel your chest off the floor to extend your lower back. Then you can practice hip hinges with a broom handle down your back as a guide to keeping back extension. If the bottom of the broom handle comes away from your backside, then your lower back is flexing.

<u>The squat pattern and the hip hinge pattern are the two major lower body exercises that will significantly improve lower body strength. Now let's look at their upper body counterparts.</u>

Horizontal Press

The bench press is a staple of upper body strength training, being the only upper body lift still used in competitive powerlifting. Horizontal pressing is the biggest exercise you can do for the front side of the shoulders. As the largest upper body barbell exercise it is also covered expansively in Starting Strength, just like the squat is. I highly recommend also reading the chapter on bench press.

There are a few points where lifters can become unstuck with the bench press. Firstly, their body position on the bench, and the position on their trunk and limbs relative to the bar and the bench. Good bench press position starts with your eyes in line with the underside of the barbell as you lay back on the bench. This should give you enough room to work clear of the hooks whilst still being close enough to re-rack the bar with minimal movement. Your feet should rest under your knees and shoulder width apart. The legs don't contribute to the force generated to move the bar but instead contribute to bracing the torso; there's no perfect foot position. Find what is comfortable for you. Avoid the temptation to bring your feet further up towards your head. This increases the arch in the lower back excessively to reduce the distance between the barbell and the chest. We are not training for a competitive bench press; you are training for an effective bench press that gives maximal stimulation of the pecs. The upper back and the back side are in contact with the bench and the arch of the lower back should be slightly exaggerated. Only to the degree of about a fist size gap between the lower back and the surface of the bench. This is created by pulling the lats and erectors down to brace the upper back towards the back of the hips.

The hooks should be positioned an inch or two below the bar when holding the bar against the supports with locked elbows. Unlocking the elbows will drop the barbell into the hooks. If you lock your elbows after the final rep, you are guaranteed to find the hooks just like you did when squatting. Unrack the bar and position it directly above the shoulders with locked elbows. Never unlock your elbows before you have reached the starting position. Doing so will slacken your arms whilst the weight is being moved over your face and throat. The bar should be held in a starting position directly above the shoulder joint. The compression forces of the barbell will transfer directly down the skeletal structure to the shoulder and the contact point with the bench. Any disruption from this position will create a moment arm and call into play one or more working muscles to cancel out these forces.

An efficient bar path is a vertical straight line down yielding to gravity under control, back up overcoming gravity with no deviation from this straight line. However, you must make some adjustments for healthy shoulder joints and to reduce the risk of injury. In the bench press the shoulder blades are pinned to the bench and are unable to move out of the way of the end of the humerus (upper arm). Therefore, the humerus must make allowances for the shoulder blade. Dropping the elbows down (towards to feet and away from the head) allows the humerus to move in a position that doesn't interfere with the shoulder blade. This interference is often referred to as impingement and occurs when two bones that shouldn't make contact, do. Keep your elbows approximately 45 degrees from your body, not up level with your shoulders, and not straight down by your sides. As the bar travels down towards the chest it should touch the middle of the sternum (breastbone) before you press it back up back to directly above the shoulder. When you unrack the bar make sure you mentally mark the position of the bar against the ceiling. Maintain focus on this point on the ceiling throughout the set ensuring that the bar comes back in line with this checkpoint at the top of each repetition.

Like the vertical press there are variations on the bench press with the barbell bench press being the default lift. Using dumbbells instead of a barbell is referred to as a dumbbell bench press. Increasing the angle of the bench changes the angle of attack and increases the contribution of the deltoids and upper portion of the pecs. An incline dumbbell bench press incorporates the change in angle and the use of dumbbells. Dumbbells can be safer because they are not connected by something - that if you get stuck- will trap you and are therefore easier to ditch if needed. Just remember that you have two independently movable pieces of equipment. Get someone capable to spot you if you are in any doubt.

Mobility is rarely an issue for the bench press. The muscles at the front of the shoulder that are used for bench pressing are the muscles that most often end up overtight. Instead of using a mobility exercise to improve your bench press I'm going to give a recommendation to ensure that the bench press you are doing doesn't make tight shoulders worse. Stretch your pecs and anterior deltoids with a doorway stretch. Walk through a doorway with your trunk upright and arms outstretched.

Also ensure you are doing at least as much horizontal pulling as pushing if not more. All your daily tasks you use your hands in front of you. It's only natural that shoulders gradually get pulled forwards. Your training should be counterbalancing this.

Horizontal pressing is balanced with horizontal pulling so let's look at horizontal pulling next.

Horizontal Pull

A healthy program will balance the upper body horizontal pressing with horizontal pulling. The main horizontal pull being a barbell bent over row. To start with feet should be a comfortable width; somewhere between hip width and shoulder width with toes turned out like a squat. To be able to get into and maintain a comfortable position for rowing you should be able to successfully complete a Romanian deadlift. That is because the bent over rowing position is like holding the lowest position in the Romanian deadlift.

The lower back should be held in extension, the natural lower back arch is maintained in the back and chest does not drop as if you are hunching over the bar. This strong back should be maintained throughout the entire set. The back should be as close to horizontal as possible because the bar path should be vertical. It is quite common for lifters to row the bar back, but this is far less efficient as the force you are lifting against is gravity and nothing else. As you will remember the further from vertical is less effective, as gravity only acts vertically. This means the bar will likely either rest on the floor between reps or just off the floor. Much higher and the back angle is too vertical.

The bar should be rowed fast into the upper stomach and lowered back to the starting position under control. If you are dipping your chest to meet the bar you are shortening the range of the movement and short-changing yourself. Not to mention whipping the bar where it is moving under its own momentum and not muscular tension, the goal is always muscular tension.

The weight of the bar will be pulling the shoulders forwards. To counter this, roll the shoulders back anticlockwise from where they naturally rest being 12 o'clock and down to 7 o'clock. Do this before taking the strain of the weight, maintain shoulder blades squeezed down and back in this position until you re rack your weights.

The grip should be a double overhand grip, underhand puts too much strain on the elbow joint and can cause tennis elbow. Being able to get the hands perfectly flat when fully supinated (upturned) is difficult for most people. Add a heavy weight and you will likely cause issues for no added benefit. If you have rounded shoulders double the volume of your horizontal pulling relative to your horizontal pressing. A simple test for shoulder mobility is if you can get your arms flat to a wall, overhead, with your back to the wall. If you can't then this is indicative of forwards rotated and tight shoulders. This can be lessened acutely with the doorway stretch. Flexibility will be improved over time by increasing the volume of rowing you do relative to pressing. As muscles only pull shorter, over time the muscles that get used the most will become the shortest. Their antagonist (opposing muscle) will be weakened as it is used less and being out muscled.

The default row is the barbell bent over row. You can replace the barbell with a pair of dumbbells and maintain the same bent over posture. You can perform a row with a single dumbbell. Rest your weight on one hand on a bench or dumbbell rack but still maintain the same posture with your legs as you would for a bent over row. Sticking one knee on a bench whilst keeping one foot on the floor is a poor position for hip and back stability so don't do it. You can perform a seated machine or cable row but you miss a lot of the benefits of the bent over position so I wouldn't necessarily trade. The temptation is to use your bodyweight as leverage, swinging your back away from the handles, creating leverage. It will move greater numbers but not improve your strength.

So that's our body in the horizontal plane, let's look next at the vertical plane.

Vertical Press

One of the oldest strength exercises. It has changed a lot from its original roots thousands of years ago, it was used as a show of strength for lifting rocks overhead. The press originally meant lifting a weight - later a barbell or dumbbell - from the floor to overhead. Give a toddler a toy barbell and the first thing they will do to show their strength is lift it above their head. Weightlifting - gaining popularity at the time - was one of only nine sports at the first modern Olympic games in 1896. The first weightlifting competition only had two events: the two-handed press and the single-handed press.

Vertical pressing develops strong and wide shoulders. This develops the medial (middle) and anterior (front) deltoids (shoulders). As a pressing exercise the triceps are strengthened at the same time. As the barbell must be balanced overhead, every muscle between the barbell and the floor is engaged to brace and hold a strong posture. Making it one of the greatest exercises for stability. If you can hold a proportion of your body weight overhead, then you will develop stability much better than by balancing on a ball ever will.

The stance for the press should be somewhere between hip width and shoulder width that is comfortable. Wide enough to help with balance but not so wide that it is uncomfortable. Never bring one foot behind as the goal is to keep the weight over the mid-foot rather than an imaginary spot somewhere between two offset feet. If you bring one foot back, you will lean back away from the bar creating a moment arm between the bar and your trunk that will work against you. Dropping one foot back is symptomatic of weak and imbalanced shoulders.

Dropping a foot back to adopt a slight split stance tilts the trunk away from the bar reducing the shoulder angle. This puts more compressive forces on the vertebrae in the lower back. The aim is to keep the feet under the body and press the weight with the weight staying over the mid foot.

Unrack the bar and take a small step away from the rack. You don't want to be more than a step away from the rack when you finish the set and are feeling fatigued. If you are tall you may need to take another step back if the barbell and plates need to clear anything on the top of the rack like chin up handles.

The movement starts with a squeeze of the glutes to push the hips forwards just enough to allow the barbell to clear your face. You want the bar to travel as close to your face as possible. The further from your face the bar is the further from your centre of gravity and mid foot it will be and the least efficient the path of the bar. Remember, for free weights the most efficient path for the weight is a straight vertical line. As soon as the bar has cleared the top of your head you will pull the rest of your upper body under the bar. Pull your hips back so that the barbell finishes above the back of the ears, with the rest of your body underneath it. Everything is resting above the mid foot. To 'lock-out' the movement to complete the rep squeeze your elbows in together and imagine they are being pulled up to create a shoulder shrug under the bar.

When the bar is moving you want to hold a strong breath, the same as you did in the squat. Take a deep breath at the bottom of each rep and hold onto it until the bar is back on your chest. Do not relax completely when breathing, keep everything tight and tense and allow a strong controlled breath.

A barbell overhead press is the standard lift, variations would then be a seated press, which uses a high incline bench and a barbell. A dumbbell press utilises dumbbells instead of a barbell but still in a standing position. Seated dumbbell presses utilise dumbbells and a high incline bench together. A single-handed press can be completed with a single dumbbell.

Although this is the bigger, in terms of muscle activation, of the two upper body pressing exercises the order of the exercises can be alternated. Find what works best for you or alternate between sessions as you prefer.

Vertical pressing is paired with vertical pulling to promote muscular and joint balance.

Vertical Pull

Like horizontal pulling, vertical pulling balances out vertical pressing. Not to mention giving stronger and wider lats. Pull ups (prone grip i.e., hands over the bar) and chin ups (supine grip i.e., hand under the bar) can be assisted with a looped resistance band. Thread it around the pull up bar and looped around the knee or foot. You can pick up these bands relatively cheaply online.

A good posture for a pull/chin up is with your shoulders rolled back to seven o'clock - as you did with the bent over row - and hands at the correct distance apart so that your forearms are vertical for most of the movement. Slightly lean back so you are pulling your chest up to meet the bar rather than the top of your head or your face.

A pull/chin up can be replaced with a pull-down machine because the resistance can be increased more gradually if you struggle to lift your body weight. When you have increased your strength significantly on the pull down you should go back to attempt the pull up. It's always a huge achievement when my clients achieve their first pull up, assisted or not. Locking your thighs under a pad and pulling a bar down is never going to have the same effect on trunk stability. Let alone the complex interaction of the chain of coordinated muscles it takes to pull your own body weight up. Pull ups will also improve greatly when you are losing fat mass as well. Muscle mass is the engine and gearbox to movement, the more you have the stronger you will be. Extra fat mass does not contribute to movement, but the added weight will make exercises harder.

Those are the four major movements of the upper body, let's now look at the calves, trunk and conditioning.

Calf Raises

Squats and hip hinges don't develop strong ankles because the ankle won't extend fully unless you lift onto your toes. Which you cannot do when squatting. The ankle range is concentrated more towards a half to a full stretch during a squat without reaching a full contraction. Calf raises are required to take the ankle to the other end of its range of movement from its normal position to fully extended (tip toes). Calf raises are strictly the only isolation exercises I will include in a whole-body plan. The benefits of incorporating calf raises are developing healthy and stable ankles. Underdeveloped calves will lead to Achilles tendon pain and an increase in ankle injuries, particularly impact movements. Most people can calf raise a lot more than they can squat because of the very short moment arm involved in a calf raised compared to a squat. Calf raises are a good exercise to practise the feeling of a very heavy weight loaded on the back. The tension in the trunk muscles must counter the large compressive forces of the barbell.

Place a barbell on the back higher than you would for a squat but still away from the neck, the bar should find a ridge of muscle to rest upon. Step one step back from the rack and squeeze your calves to raise up onto the balls of your feet and lower back down under control. You can use a safety bar - a thick padded bar with handles - if you struggle maintaining balance and need to steady yourself with one hand. But go slow and steady and you should be able to balance after the first few sets.

Trunk

When you think of the trunk you often think of the core, and we think of the core as rectus abdominis or the six-pack muscles. This is because most people based their training on what fitness models were doing in the 80s and it stuck. The core technically covers everything from the armpits to the tops of the knees. The lumbopelvic hip complex - the lower back and the hips - is a major part of this that often gets overlooked. Too much emphasis on the muscles that create flexion of the hips causes injury.

Contrary to what you have been taught about the core, the role of the core is often to resist the trunk being extended rather than to generate flexion. I prefer plank or rollout movements more than sit up movements. The only sit up movement that I prescribe is a full sit up where the trunk is moving through 90 degrees to vertical to engage the erectors and the flexors. To perform a plank, lie on your front on the floor with your toes under your ankles and your elbows under your shoulders. Lift into a plank from the floor, don't sag down into a plank. The plank is a perfect opportunity to practise being more conscious of your posture, maintaining a relatively straight back. Allowing for a healthy arch in your lower back and shoulders rolled back. You can develop a plank to a side plank, or to a rollout but it's important to still maintain your best posture. The idea is to challenge your posture in a safe environment, not completely disregard it.

Conditioning

Conditioning is a key part of a resistance program in addition to the cardiovascular work you will be doing. This gives you a better 'training engine'. The goal here is to spike your heart rate during the session, this can be very effective when - facilities allowing - the session is completed as a circuit. Each round the heart rate will be elevated to close to maximum.

Pick any cardio machine that is in easy reach in the gym. Set a timer; anything between 30 seconds and 120 seconds will do and then try to achieve the greatest distance possible in that time. (You can swap time for calories if that motivates you more). The goal is to beat the distance each time. You will be able to achieve a greater distance as your conditioning improves.

These are all the exercises of the whole-body program. Let's now look at the additional exercises that we include in the split programs.

Leg Extension

A leg extension machine is loading the front of the shank (shin) of the leg and using the moment arm of the shin bone like the paddle lever. The axis is the centre of the knee that rotation occurs in, the force is applied from the quadriceps down the patella tendon to the Tibia. The leg extension should only be used as an accessory to the squat because the quadriceps cross over the front of the hip as well as the front of the knee. During a leg extension you are fixing the hip, holding it stationary, whilst you extend the knee.

Other exercises that stimulate the quadriceps can be substituted. Look for any exercise that keeps the leg loaded and flexes the knee to 90 degrees or more. Bulgarian split squats and step up are two of my favourites.

Leg Curl

The leg curl is the opposite movement at the knee to the leg extension. The knee is flexed by the hamstring which is shortened at the bottom end whilst being held stationary at the top end as you lay flat on the bench. Like leg extensions most of the work should be done with a deep squat and a hip hinge. Isolation exercises provide additional volume to assist these larger exercises.

To perform a leg curl well, push the front of your hips into the bench to avoid lifting your hips off the bench. This happens so the hips shorten the range of motion and reduce the moment. Keep the resistance light enough that you can control the tempo and technique.

You can substitute other exercises that also flex the knee. Any Nordic hamstring exercise where the lower leg is fixed, and the knee extends eccentrically, or hip hinge exercise is a good substitute.

Elbow Flexion

Better known as bicep curls. You train your biceps every time you do a row or a pull up, but with increased training frequency you can now target the biceps specifically. The biceps are one of many muscles that cross two joints. The biceps cross over the shoulder and the elbow joint, not just the elbow joint as many would assume. This means that the biceps can raise the upper arm as well as raise the lower arm. The goal of a biceps curl is to maximally squeeze the elbow joint closed. Beware that the biceps can shorten when the elbows are raised disrupting the bicep curl movement. When weights are too heavy to curl, the shoulder shortens the bicep without the biceps curling, cutting off vital biceps curl range.

Bicep curls can be done with barbells, EZ bars - which have a more forgiving angled grip to take the strain off elbows when the hands are supinated - or dumbbells which allow for a variety of techniques. You can complete them standing, seated, or even using a preacher bench to fix your upper arms. Whichever you prefer is fine if you remember the goal is to close the elbow joint fully. Fixing the upper arm will assist with this because it takes away the upper arm swing that will work against you. For every bit that the momentum of swing moves the weight your muscles aren't.

Everyone loves training biceps, have fun here. Set yourself a challenge, or feel free to break free from the usual structure of sets and reps. Just focus on squeezing the gap inside the elbow closed.

Elbow Extension

If the biceps flex the elbow, then the triceps extend it. To fully engage the triceps the elbow joint needs to be straightened fully and locked at the top. This is perfectly safe because the resistance is acting perpendicular to the moment arm; in this instance it's the forearm. There are three heads to the triceps, but which means they typically have about 150% of the mass of the biceps and are stronger.

The goal of triceps extensions is to keep the upper arm still. The triceps also cross both the shoulder and elbow joints. Excessive movement will take the stimulus away from the triceps or will act to lengthen the triceps when you are trying to shorten them.

If you have tight shoulders, and you are on a split program, increase the volume of triceps compared to biceps. Tight shoulders often mean short biceps. Just like biceps triceps extensions can be completed using a barbell, EZ bar or dumbbells. Some people might find that trying to grip a straight bar is tough with fully pronated hands like with a barbell skull crusher.

Both biceps curls and triceps extensions are flexion and extension of the elbow joint and therefore require a stationary upper arm for efficient and effective rotation of the elbow joint. The more you can isolate this movement the more of the movement you are generating from the target muscles. That's why these isolation exercises don't appear in the full body plan. A novice trainer should spend time experimenting with positions and movements to feel the effect any slight deviations have before trying to harness specific movement into isolation exercises. Rushing through any of this without mastering movement means focusing on shifting a weight from A to B rather than using the weight as a tool to stimulate a specific muscle in a specific way.

Flyes/Raises

During chest flyes the upper arm is moving in the same fashion as with a bench press, but with an extended lever out past the elbow to the hand, rather than the hand sitting above the elbow. The further the hand moves away from the body the greater the moment arm acting on it and the weight (remember the pedal on your bike?). This is why flyes feel progressively harder as the weight is lowered and easier as the weight is raised. There is no tension on the pecs when the weight is resting directly above the shoulder. The force is being transferred through the bones of the arm as a compressive force. But you are well versed in this now.

Flyes and raises make the most of long levers, hence they must be completed with relatively lighter weights; approximately half of the weight that you would press with. The lever is half the length (moment arm from the shoulder to the elbow instead of from the shoulder to the hand). Half the weight with a lever that is twice the length generates the same moment.

One of the greatest mistakes I see with flyes is bringing the weight inside, or past the vertical at the top of the rep. This will deload the pecs because the pecs are only being tensioned when the lever is pulling on them. Just like the action of a drawbridge. For the tension to be on a muscle the lever must be leaning out a degree or more from the vertical in a direction away from the muscle.

Raises use the medial deltoids the same as vertical presses. Raises can be substituted in for vertical press or can be used for additional volume.

Now you know what exercises we will be including in the plan. How will you test our strength going forwards?

TESTING STRENGTH

Strength is how much force you can generate. Maximum strength is the maximum amount of force you - or for that matter one or more of your muscles - can generate. Measuring force directly requires an expensive dynamometer. You make assumptions based on the weight you lift. As you lift more weight, you are generating more force. If you remember; force = mass multiplied by acceleration (squared), if the tempo stays constant, as weight increases so too does the force created by the muscle.

The traditional way to test strength is by testing a one repetition maximum. As intensity increases volume decreases so the closest you can get to maximum force is one successful repetition. You can then compare all other repetition ranges to this absolute.

I spent the first few years of my career working with professional rugby players in the UK. One of the first things I learned is that we don't spend time testing when we could be training! Rarely in training do you use single reps to failure as these sets are the most taxing on the nervous system. We had to use tests that could be done in training without any significant interruption. By taking one set on one exercise to failure, a repetition maximum (RM), you can then *theoretically* estimate a one-repetition maximum (1RM) for that exercise. Two common formulae for estimating 1RM are as follows[15]:

Epley formula

$$1RM = Weight\ (kg) \times (1 + 0.0333 \times Reps)$$

Lombardi formula

$$1RM = (Weight\ (kg) \times Reps)^{0.1}$$

---

[15] Hughes, V. A., Frontera, W. R., Wood, M., Evans, W. J., Dallal, G. E., Roubenoff, R., & Singh, M. A. F. (2001). Accuracy of seven equations for predicting 1RM performance of apparently healthy sedentary older adults. *Journal of Aging and Physical Activity, 9*(3), 357–366. https://doi.org/10.1123/japa.9.3.357

By predicting a 1RM you get an indication of the maximum potential you should be able to achieve on any given day. As your strength work will vary in intensity and volume this gives you a standardised comparison of the same lifts.

If you don't want to take every exercise to failure, then you need a way to compare non-maximal and maximal sets. 'Reps in reserve' is a simple system to record how close you are to failure. Zero reps in reserve for maximal sets. Then you estimate from one or more reps in reserve for how many reps you think you would have been able to complete had you continued. You can use .5 increments if you're unsure between reps. You can factor reps in reserve into the above equation to predict 1RM successfully at submaximal intensities. Let's say you lifted 105 kilograms for four repetitions.

Epley formula

$$1RM = Weight\ (kg) \times (1 + 0.0333 \times (Reps$$
$$+ Reps\ in\ Reserve)$$

Lombardi formula

$$1RM = (Weight\ (kg) \times Reps + Reps\ in\ Reserve)^{0.1}$$

Let's say you lifted 105 kilograms for four repetitions.

Epley formula

$$1RM = 105 \times (1 + 0.0333 \times 4) = 119kg$$

Lombardi formula

$$1RM = (105 \times 4)^{0.1} = 121kg$$

You would get the same numbers if you factored reps in reserve into the equation if you were able to successfully predict how near to failure you are.

The error of being one repetition higher or lower only has a knock-on effect of being approximately +/- 2.5% so we're not overly concerned if this isn't perfect. It is useful to give an idea if we are progressing by standardising the loads we are lifting. I use this as a standardised score on my major lifts. It can't be used on body weight exercises where the weight cannot be graded. If you want to compare your squat across weeks where you've managed different weights, reps, and reps in reserve it gives you a good enough eyeball on the progress you've made. That is what's most important here. This is a tool to monitor progress, not perfectly estimate 1RM. Let's take a bench press for example. If you lift 105kg for 2 reps with 2 reps in reserve, you're assuming had you pushed it you would have performed four reps. With the benefit of not having the fatigue that comes with going for the maximal nine reps. This is useful when you are monitoring your training. Not doing specific testing sessions. If the following week you lift 107.5kg for 2 reps with one rep in reserve, then your theoretical 1RM would be between 118kg and 120kg. No big deal from one session to the next but you can keep an eye on your numbers over time and expect for them to be creeping upwards.

Epley formula

$$1RM = 107.5 \times \big(1 + 0.0333 \times (2 + 1)\big) = 118kg$$

Lombardi formula

$$1RM = \left(107.5 \times (2 + 1)\right)^{0.1} = 120kg$$

Bear in mind that accuracy decreases the more reps you do because the theoretical 1RM is being based on a number that is further away from the actual 1RM. That's just statistics; if I surveyed 1,000 people versus 1,000,000 people, I would get a better representation of the country with the sample of 1,000,000 people.

This is a simple way to compare your performance in the gym over several weeks where the number of repetitions you are doing often vary, but you spare yourself from pushing to exhaustion on every exercise. Feel free to try a 1RM every now and then if you are so inclined and can do it safely. This is a simple 'set and forget' column you can add into your training log. It is one more piece of information that will help guide your training. You can set this up by copying the above formula and adding a column into an excel sheet if you track your weights, reps, and reps in reserve. Or go to https://intelligentshedder.com/tools where I have done all

the hard work for you, and you can steal my training log.

That's strength covered, let's look at endurance next.

TESTING ENDURANCE

Kenneth H. Cooper, dubbed the father of aerobics, coined the term aerobics in his 1968 book of the same name. He devised a simple test to test cardiovascular fitness in the US Air Force. The Cooper 12-minute run is the gold standard of endurance testing. The Cooper 12-minute run test is a simple time trial. The further you can run in twelve minutes the greater your fitness. 12-minute run time has a 90% correlation with VO_2max[16]; how much oxygen your body can utilise. The more oxygen your body can utilise the better endurance you have.

---

[16] Cooper, K. H. (1968) A means of assessing maximal oxygen uptake. Journal of the American Medical Association 203:201-204.

Distance (m)	Time	Who?	Average Speed (m/s)
100	9.58s	Usain Bolt	10.44
200	19.19s	Usain Bolt	10.42
200	19.92s	Frank Fredericks	10.04
400	43.03s	Wayne Van Niekerk	9.30
400	44.57s	Kerron Clement	8.97
800	1:40.91	David Rudisha	7.93
800	1:42.67	Wilson Kipketer	7.79
1,000	2:11.96	Noah Ngeny	7.58
1,000	2:14.20	Ayanleh Souleiman	7.45
1,500	3:26.00	Hicham El Guerrouj	7.28
1,500	3:30.60	Jakob Ingebrigtsen	7.12
1,609.34	3:43.13	Hicham El Guerrouj	7.21
1,609.34	3:47.01	Yomif Kejelcha	7.09
1,609.34	3:56.13	Hobbs Kessler	6.82
1,609.34	3:54.60	Emmanuel Wanyonyi	6.86
2,000	4:43.13	Jakob Ingebrigtsen	7.06
3,000	7:20.67	Daniel Komen	6.81
3,000	7:23.81	Lamecha Girma	6.76
5,000	12:35.36	Joshua Cheptegei	6.62
5,000	12:49.00	Berihu Aregawi	6.50
5,000	12:49.60	Kenenisa Bekele	6.50
10,000	26:11.00	Joshua Cheptegei	6.37
10,000	26:24.00	Rhonex Kipruto	6.31
21,097	57:31.00	Jacob Kiplimo	6.11
21,330	1:00:00.00	Mo Farah	5.93
42,194	2:00:35.00	Kelvin Kiptum	5.83
50,000	2:38:43.00	CJ Albertson	5.25

Above you'll see the current list of world records in track athletics (track, indoor and road included). These are the same world records I used in the energy systems chapter. If you connect the dots across all the world records this shows you the current maximum human potential. If you could build a superhuman that could run at current perfection this is what it would look like. Using this theoretical superhuman to calculate the best 12-minute Cooper test result, it would be closest to Joshua Cheptegei's 5km time of 12:35.36. Average for a man in his 30s is 2,200m in 12 minutes, if you're in your 40s it's closer to 1,900m. In all fairness Joshua Cheptegei is in his twenties, and currently the world's greatest 5k runner. The average man running for 12 minutes will be expected to achieve 51.7% of what Joshua Cheptegei can. If we use this to estimate Joshua Cheptegei's VO_2max he will have an approximate VO_2max of 88.07ml/kg/min. This means he can breathe in, and his muscles can use 5.46 litres of oxygen every minute he is running. Given the partial pressure of oxygen is approximately 21% he would have to breathe in 22 litres of air every minute to maintain his running speed.

To calculate your own VO₂max you can use the following equation using the distance you covered running for 12 minutes:

$$VO_2 max = \frac{Distance(m) - 504.9}{44.73}$$

There is a similar formula if you run a mile and a half instead of 12 minutes.

$$VO_2 max = \frac{483}{Time \ (mins)} + 3.5$$

Endurance tests shouldn't stand outside of regular training, just the same as strength testing. Instead, tests should be incorporated into your program. The training itself becomes the test. Repeat the test and if you can beat your time then your cardiovascular fitness is improving. You can always mix it up and test the distance you can reach in a set time instead. The two are related. There is no perfect time or distance to test over. You can test over one kilometre or twenty, it doesn't matter if you are testing yourself.

By testing for both strength and endurance you are testing your capabilities at both ends of the fitness spectrum. The maximum force you can generate and how long you can keep going. I wouldn't worry about any other fitness tests other than these. Both these tests represent absolute capacities. If both are increased it will signify increased fitness for sure.

To create a repeatable endurance test without adding extra work to your training there are just a few numbers you need to familiarise yourself with.

Speed versus Pace

Speed is distance divided by time. How fast something moves is the product of how much distance it covers in a specific time. Speed = Distance / Time. You can rotate each of these around to change the formula, meaning if you know two of them you can calculate the third. Visually this is usually represented like the below illustration where d = distance, t = time and s = speed.

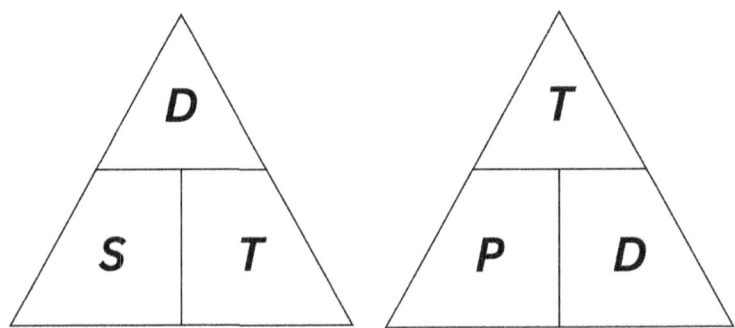

Use the above in the following way: multiply the two factors on the bottom to get the top factor e.g., speed x time = distance. Divide the top factor by one of the bottom factors to get the other bottom factor e.g., time ÷ pace = distance.

Keeping the distance constant and targeting time as your goal, this is in effect a function of speed; distance / time. This would be like choosing to run 5km and aiming for a quicker time each time. The opposite: time / distance is pace. A high speed is covering a greater distance in less time and a faster pace is taking less time to cover more distance.

$$\frac{Distance}{Time} = Speed \quad \frac{Time}{Distance} = Pace$$

You will often hear runners talk about their pace per mile or kilometre. Pace is simply speed flipped the other way. Endurance training is an attempt over time to increase speed and quicken pace. As speed is the inverse of pace and *vice versa* to improve one would improve the other by the same degree.

$$\frac{\uparrow Distance}{\downarrow Time} = \uparrow Speed \quad \frac{\downarrow Time}{\uparrow Distance} = \downarrow Pace$$

5,000m in 20 minutes would be a speed of 15km/h and a pace of 4 minutes per kilometre. An improvement of 2 minutes over 5km would be an increase of speed by a further 1.667km/h.

To improve your endurance, it doesn't matter what mode you use, get out there and run, cycle, swim or handstand walk! Measure distance and time, vary the two to keep it interesting but keep a log of your speed and pace to track improvements.

That's everything for the training section. In the next chapter I have provided some example training plans.

YOUR TRAINING PLAN

Here are all three session plans in one place. For a digital copy go to https://intelligentshedder.com/tools

There is a minimum of one session; the whole-body program and a maximum of three sessions; the split program. The whole-body program is one session (session one) repeated twice for a total of three sessions per week. The upper/lower split has two sessions (sessions one and two) to be repeated once for a total of four sessions per week. The upper push, upper pull, legs split has three sessions (sessions one, two and three) to be repeated once for a total of six sessions per week.

Session One

WB	Order	Lower	Order	Sets	Reps	Rest
Squat	A1	Squat	A1	1-4	8-12	30s
Hip hinge	B1	Hip hinge	B1	1-4	8-12	30s
Hor. Press	C1	Knee Extension	C1	1-4	8-12	30s
Hor. Pull	D1	Knee Flexion	C2	1-4	8-12	30s
Vertical Press	E1	Calf Raises	D1	1-4	8-12	30s
Vertical Pull	F1	Trunk	D2	1-4	8-12	30s
Trunk	G1			1-4	8-12	30s
Calf Raises	H1			1-4	8-12	30s
Conditioning	I1	Conditioning	D3	1-4	30-90s	120s

Session Two

Upper	Order	Press	Order	Sets	Reps	Rest
Horizontal Press	A1	Horizontal Press	A1	1-4	8-12	30s
Horizontal Pull	B1	Vertical Press	B1	1-4	8-12	30s
Vertical Press	C1	Elbow Extension	C1	1-4	8-12	30s
Vertical Pull	D1	Pec Flyes	C2	1-4	8-12	30s
Elbow Flexion	E1	Lateral Raises	C3	1-4	8-12	30s
Elbow Extension	F1			1-4	8-12	30s
Rear Deltoids	G1			1-4	8-12	30s
	H1			1-4	30-90s	120s

Session Three

Pull	Order	Sets	Reps	Rest
Horizontal Row	A1	1-4	8-12	30s
Pull/Chin ups	B1	1-4	8-12	30s
Elbow Flexion	C1	1-4	8-12	30s
Rear Delt Flyes	C2	1-4	8-12	30s
Straight Arm Pulldown	C3	1-4	8-12	120s

CONCLUSION

Everything in fitness is measurable. This simple truth holds the key to achieving consistent, sustainable progress and avoiding the all-too-common cycles of boom and bust. Whether you aim to lose fat, build muscle, or improve your endurance, the foundation lies in identifying what can be tracked, monitored, and adjusted.

When we measure something, we give it clarity. Whether it's your weight, body fat percentage, or the weight of your lifts, each data point represents a stepping stone on your journey. Without these measurements, fitness often feels like a guessing game - one that leads to frustration and burnout. When you have a scorecard, however, you transform your approach into one of accountability and precision.

But measurement alone isn't enough; the true magic lies in using this data to guide moderate, consistent adjustments. There's no need for extreme swings in your training or nutrition. Instead, small, consistent changes, 1% improvements, compound over time into dramatic results. This approach not only prevents burnout but also creates habits that you can sustain for life.

The reason most people fail is that they rely on motivation, which ebbs and flows. Consistency, however, is fuelled by the knowledge that every effort you put in is contributing to measurable progress. Fitness doesn't have to be an all-or-nothing endeavour. You can improve your physique, your strength, and your health with a steady, controlled approach. No more "starting over" every January.

The mindset shift is simple but profound: view your fitness journey as an ongoing series of experiments. Measure, adjust, and refine. Celebrate the small wins and use setbacks as opportunities to learn and recalibrate. Fitness is not a destination; it's a continuous process, guided by data and driven by commitment.

As you close this book, remember, anything measurable can be changed. Progress, no matter how incremental, is still progress. Embrace this principle, you're not just transforming your body. You're transforming your relationship with health and fitness. This isn't the end of your journey; it's the beginning of a smarter, more sustainable path forward. Keep measuring, keep adjusting, and most importantly, keep going.

BONUS CHAPTER: THE IMPORTANCE OF ACCOUNTABILITY

Accountability is a powerful, often underestimated factor in achieving your fitness goals. It keeps you focused, motivated, and consistent as you work toward transforming your body and health. In fact, research shows that having an 'accountability buddy' gives you a 65% chance of achieving your goal. Having regular accountability check-ins, for example hiring a coach to check in with weekly, greatly improves your likelihood of success to 95%. You are far more likely to achieve a goal when you have accountability systems in place.

Having someone you're accountable to means you're less likely to skip workouts, ignore your nutrition plan, or lose focus on your goals. When there's someone invested in your success, you gain an extra layer of motivation that helps keep you committed. Especially on those days when enthusiasm may wane.

Let me take a minute to introduce the 'Intelligent Shedder Program'. With the Intelligent Shedder Program at https://intelligentshedder.com/join, you can get this powerful support. Our online coaching system is designed to adapt to your lifestyle, providing accountability check-ins, guidance, and motivation wherever you are in the world. This flexibility is ideal if you travel or have a busy schedule that makes it hard to commit to a traditional fitness plan.

Professional accountability with a knowledgeable online coach provides a structured system that allows you to:

Stay Consistent

With regular progress check-ins, you'll receive the encouragement you need to keep going and stay committed, no matter where life takes you.

Adapt Your Plan Flexibly

Life changes, and so can your plan. With the Intelligent Shedder program, your coach can adjust your workout and nutrition plans based on your circumstances, helping you maintain progress even when your schedule or location changes.

Receive Expert Guidance

Beyond motivation, professional accountability ensures you're following a tailored plan created by someone with the knowledge and experience to help you reach your goals.

Gain a Supportive Partner

Your coach is there to celebrate your wins, help you overcome obstacles, and keep you motivated, making your journey less about discipline alone and more about support and encouragement.

If you're ready to transform your fitness journey with accountability that's tailored to fit your life, join the Intelligent Shedder Program. We understand that flexibility is essential, which is why our online coaching allows you to check in and receive support wherever you are—whether you're at home, on the road, or travelling internationally.

MY READING LIST

This list is not exhaustive but without being able to credit them directly because I haven't used their information directly in writing this book, they have however all shaped my outlook on health and fitness so deserve a special mention.

1. Advances in Functional Training - Michael Boyle

2. Always Hungry - David Ludwig

3. Atomic Habits - James Clear

4. Back Mechanic - Dr. Stuart McGill

5. Becoming A Supple Leopard - Dr. Kelly Starrett & Glen Cordoza

6. Chop Wood, Carry Water - Joshua Medcalf

7. Don't Believe Everything You Think - Joseph Nguyen

8. Find Your Why - Simon Sinek

9. Gene Eating - Dr. Giles Yeo

10. Grit - Angela Duckworth

11. In Defence of Food - Michael Pollan

12. Living With A Seal - Jesse Itzler

13. Mindset - Carol Dweck

14. Start With Why - Simon Sinek

15. Starting Strength: Basic Barbell Training - Mark

Rippertoe

16. Supertraining - Mel C. Siff

17. The Complete Contest Prep Guide - Layne Norton

18. The Gold's Gym Mass Building Training & Nutrition

System - Grymkowski, Conners, Kimber & Reynolds

19. The Gold's Gym Training Encyclopaedia -

Grymkowski, Conners, Kimber & Reynolds

20. The Muscle and Strength Pyramid (Nutrition) - Eric

Helms

21. The Muscle and Strength Pyramid (Training) - Eric

Helms

22. The New Encyclopaedia of Modern Bodybuilding -

Arnold Schwarzenegger

23. The Power of Habits - Charles Duhigg

24. The Wim Hoff Method - Wim Hoff

25. The World's Fittest Book - Ross Edgeley

26. Ultimate Bodybuilding - Joe Weider

27. Why We Sleep - Matthew Walker

28. Your Ultimate Body Transformation Guide - Nick Mitchell

29. Zen Mind, Beginner's Mind - Shunryu Suzuki

Printed in Great Britain
by Amazon

58543968R00198